The
Secret
Strength
of
Depression

The Secret Strength of Depression

by
Frederic F. Flach, M.D.

J. B. Lippincott Company
Philadelphia and New York

Published by arrangement with Bantam Books, Inc.

U.S. Library of Congress Cataloging in Publication Data

Flach, Frederic F
  The secret strength of depression.

  Bibliography: p.
  1. Depression, Mental. I. Title. [DNLM: 1. Depression—Popular works. WM207 F571s 1974]
RC537.F56   616.8′528   74–3097
ISBN–0–397–01031–1

Lines from "The Death of the Hired Man" are quoted from
The Poetry of Robert Frost, edited by Edward Connery Lathem.
Copyright 1930, 1939, © 1969 by Holt, Rinehart and Winston, Inc.
Copyright © 1958 by Robert Frost. Copyright © 1967 by Lesley
Frost Ballantine. Reprinted by permission of Holt, Rinehart and
Winston, Inc.

Lines from *The Cocktail Party* by T. S. Eliot are quoted by
permission of Harcourt Brace Jovanovich, Inc., and Faber and
Faber Ltd.

TO MY CHILDREN

*who have kept me in touch
with the way things are
in a changing world*

Author's Note

A BOOK is usually written not once but many times. In the preparation of this manuscript, I owe sincere thanks to the editors whose advice and direction helped shape its character: Grace Bechtold of Bantam Books for her enthusiastic and continued support; Beatrice Rosenfeld of J. B. Lippincott Company for her precise and careful clarifications; and Wilhemina Marvel for her creative and incisive editorial contributions throughout the writing of the book. I also wish to thank Dr. Oskar Diethelm, Emeritus Professor of Psychiatry at Cornell University Medical College, for reviewing the material for historical and scientific accuracy and for uncovering the seventeenth-century treatise on melancholia by my namesake, Fridericus Flacht, in the archives of the University of Basel in Switzerland.

The men and women described throughout the pages of the book are people I have encountered over the twenty-year period in which I have been practicing psychiatry and training residents in psychiatry. The patients' names and certain details regarding their life situations have been changed to preserve their anonymity.

Contents

The
Secret
Strength
of
Depression

1
The
Nature
of
Depression

THERE IS A STRONG WIND called the mistral that blows across the south of France—a dry and chilling current of air that brings with it a sharp rise in the incidence of depression. In Bavaria, a warm wind called *der Föhn* blows north from the Alps when the snows melt; as it descends on Munich, the suicide rate increases for a period of several days. For many people Christmas is traditionally associated with a mood of heightened sadness and loneliness; spring, too, is a time when depression is common. Common, also, are what are known as anniversary reactions—depressed moods that recur at the same time of year as events that in prior years had been upsetting: "Two years ago this month my father died," or "Last year at this time I was going through the worst part of the divorce."

Depression is not limited to specific times and places, however, because it is essentially a reaction to stress. Hence, depression is a mood that can occur *at any time to anyone.* It is safe to assume that at least one-half of the adult population in the United States has been depressed at one time or another. In fact, it has been estimated that at any given moment, approximately eight million Americans are in immediate need of professional help for depression. Unfortunately, the majority of these people are not aware of their depression.

One reason so many people fail to recognize depression is that it is often confused with ordinary unhappiness. There are circumstances in everyone's life that cause some unhappiness. To be unhappy is to be sad or discontented when things go wrong; it does not involve a loss of perspective. Being depressed, on the other hand, is a mood which affects a person's basic emotional disposition, determining how he experiences and perceives himself and his surroundings. "There's a real difference between being unhappy and being depressed," commented one man in therapy. "When my wife and I have an occasional argument, I'm unhappy about it. I don't like it. But it's part of living. We make up in a fairly short time. I may be concerned over it, but I can sleep all right, and I still feel in good spirits.

"But when I'm depressed, that's a different matter. It hurts all over. It's almost something physical. I can't get to sleep at night, and I can't sleep through the night. Even though there are still times when I'm in pretty good spirits, the mood comes over me nearly every day. It colors the way I look at everything. If my wife and I have a fight, our marriage seems hopeless. If I have a business problem, which I would normally react to with some tension and frustration but which I would deal with promptly and appropriately, I feel as though I'm really a lousy businessman and I battle with the problem of self-confidence instead of just dealing with the issues in front of me."

The difficulty in recognizing depression is strongly reinforced by popular misconceptions about the nature of depression. Although many people commonly speak of themselves as depressed, they do not mean that they are really depressed, since they believe that true depression is a serious mental illness. Fearful of the implications of mental illness, they consider depression to be exclusively a severe condition that may be part of the manic-depressive cycle or that seriously incapacitates people, forcing them to be hospitalized. But only a small segment of the vast pool of depressed individuals is represented by such dramatic instances of depression. The great majority of depressed individuals experience comparatively mild forms of the condition, dangerous but readily ignored. As a result, it is often difficult for most of them to identify with the more serious illustrations of melancholia. And so, to them, depression is something that happens to someone else.

Furthermore, being depressed in the face of stress is still considered by a large number of people as a mark of weakness and hence a source of embarrassment. In short, many of us would prefer to ignore signs of depression, rather than to acknowledge that *the only healthy reaction to many life situations is depression.*

Becoming depressed is a common psychobiological response to stress. In the course of a lifetime, every human being must cope with a multitude of stresses. Because man is a psychobiological unit, with every thought and feeling producing a correlative change in the chemistry of the nervous system, he will react to, and cope with, stress on both a physical and psychological plane. Hence a severe viral infection may trigger a period of mental depression, and the death of a loved one may produce feelings of depression that have physical components. Because man is also a social being, his reaction will affect his environment and will, in turn, be affected by the response from the environment.

Ordinary, day-to-day fluctuations in mood can be viewed as mild episodes of depression. Nearly everyone has moments of experiencing a sense of futility, of being more sensitive than usual, of crying easily. The characteristic signs of depression include a lowering in spirits, difficulty in sleeping, a loss of self-esteem, and a loss of perspective. Other changes associated with depression include fatigue, a loss of energy, a desire to avoid being with people, lowered sexual desire and ability, poor appetite and weight loss, hypersensitivity, fearfulness and irritability, and physical complaints without any diagnosable basis. Rarely do they all occur together. More often, one or another sign is prominent—sexual difficulties, for example. When the psychiatric outpatient department of a major university hospital established a sex therapy clinic, re-

quests for treatment increased from a few hundred a
month for previously offered therapy services to nearly
two thousand a month for sex therapy alone. The majority of these applicants were found to be suffering
from some degree of depression.

Many people do not realize that they are depressed because they fail to make a connection
between the one or two signs of depression that they
have noticed and the over-all change in their mood.
Because they don't consider jumping out of windows
or overdosing themselves with sleeping pills, they are
unable to see that they may be as affected by depression as others who, in a severe and acute reaction to
stress, experience weeks of fear and despondency, falling apart in a paradoxical effort to cope and not cope
at the same time.

Depressive reactions can arbitrarily be divided
into two forms: an *acute*, immediate type and a more
enduring or *chronic* type. Acute depression is a short-
lived, intense, painful, directly experienced change of
mood from which the individual can usually recover
in a reasonable period of time. It may run on for weeks
and even months, but as a rule the intensity and duration
of the reaction are appropriate to the nature of the
events causing it. While it would be clearly inappropriate to become deeply depressed after two or three job
rejections, a period of depression lasting six months or
more following a divorce would be quite natural.

An acute depressive reaction may be extremely
mild: a few hours of sadness, a transient feeling of
being rejected, a day or two of disappointment. It
may become intense when the stress giving rise to it is

serious and the person experiencing it is especially sensitive to that stress. A forty-two-year-old woman became acutely depressed after her mother and her eighteen-year-old son were killed in an automobile accident. She was beside herself. She could not sleep, refused to eat, and would not talk with anyone. She often thought of wanting to die. With medical help, she pulled out of the more intense phase of her re-action in a few months and gradually learned to come to terms with the disastrous happenings. Her acute reaction, painful and disruptive as it had been, pro-tected her from becoming chronically and bitterly depressed.

Acute depressive episodes serve as an outlet for strong feelings and, as such, are a necessary and de-sirable way of reacting to certain major life changes, such as loss. Some events—loss of employment, death of a husband or wife, serious illness in a child—are clearly threatening to most people. The termination of a love relationship or marriage is equally likely to set off a depression, particularly when the element of per-sonal rejection is added. The doubling of the divorce rate in the last ten years, for instance, has made family disruption a common trigger for depression in chil-dren as well as parents. The extent of an individual's reaction to a particular loss is determined by his per-sonality. Certain people will be more affected by loss as a result of childhood experiences, as in the case of a person who, while still very young, lost one or both parents through death or divorce.

In addition to the connection between depression and loss, a sufficient number of stresses occurring within a limited time frame can evoke a depressive reaction in almost anyone, as has been pointed out by psychiatrist Eugene Paykel and others. Nor do these events have to be exclusively misfortunes. If, for example, a man receives an important promotion and is transferred to a new part of the country, loses a large sum of money in the stock market, and attends the college graduation of his only child, all in a few months' time, he is likely to become somewhat depressed—a natural response to cumulative stress. His reaction may well be puzzling to himself and others because most of these changes could generally be thought of as good.

In other words, a series of major changes, for better or worse, compacted into a small enough span of time is apt to produce depression in most people. The relevance of such a finding to this society, replete as it is with disruption in life patterns and values, is at once apparent.

The human being must react psychobiologically to stress. Too great a response, and too little, are equally problematic. If no reaction at all is apparent in the face of a critical stress, the individual should be suspected of blocking out depression. He runs a high risk of a delayed reaction occurring months later, or of entering the chronic and more insidious form of depression. Chronic depression may also be the aftermath of an acute depression which the person has not had the resilience or insight to cope with successfully.

In contrast to acute depression, which affords one an opportunity for insight, chronic depression is nearly always disabling and will complicate the person's life in ways that may be hard to correct and may at times be irreversible. The immobilizing quality of the mood change persists, as if the nervous system continues to short-circuit, reinforcing again and again its crippling effect. The signs of chronic depression are similar to those of acute depression: low self-esteem, a high degree of personal sensitivity, insomnia, withdrawal, a low tolerance for criticism, difficulty in making decisions, a tendency to put things off. There is a strong urge to rationalize the depression. "I work too hard," commented a thirty-four-year-old store manager. "With three kids at home, I don't have any time to myself; that's why I'm tired all the time." The tendency is to project onto the immediate environment the causes for the loss of drive or energy. People fifty years of age or older will regard the slow, insidious personality change as a part of the process of "getting older," as if feelings of futility and immobilization were necessarily part of aging.

Chronic depression can be difficult to identify because it is long-standing and more subtle than acute depression, and because it seems to be a part of the person's temperament or personality rather than a mood. "He's a pessimist, a born worrier," said one woman in describing her depressed father. In some people the only evidence of chronic depression may be a persistent or recurring nervousness and tension, which is unrelieved by mild tranquilizers or recreation. During a vacation, away from ordinary pressures, the person in an acute depression often feels a sustained lifting in mood. By contrast, the chronically depressed individual may, in fact, feel worse while he is away; even if he does experience some relief, he will rapidly re-enter his depression when he returns to his usual life situation. The key to chronic depression is its persistence; it will not go away by itself.

The exact point at which a chronic depression may have begun is hard to spot. Unlike acute depression, the chronic form is usually detached from its causes in the person's mind. Feelings which should have been experienced at the time of the stressful events may have been denied, blocked out. Sometimes people may even be misled into being "proud" of how calmly they seemed to have handled a particular misfortune. The importance of the causal events may escape notice because the person failed to become sufficiently upset by them at the time.

A case in point is a twenty-four-year-old man who was quite upset because he felt that he had made a serious error in his choice of careers. He had studied to be a marine biologist, but had quit six months before fulfilling the requirements for his doctorate to take a job teaching at a private high school. Within a few months he again left his work, this time returning to his parents' home. There he was frequently silent and morose. He and his family spent hours going over and over ideas about his career dilemma without arriving at any solutions.

At no time did anyone recognize that he had really been depressed prior to ending his studies and that the original trigger for his depression was rejection. His girl friend, with whom he had been deeply involved for several years, had abruptly ended the relationship some time earlier. He seemed to have taken the rejection in stride, and there was nearly a year's delay between this event and his quitting his graduate program.

This kind of delay between the change responsible for the depression and the first evidence of a change in mood is common in chronic depression. Because the mood change is not recognized for what it is, other problems *caused by* the depression can become paramount. Marital problems, financial difficulties, sexual frustrations, and many other conflicts often result from the effect the chronic mood has over the person experiencing it. Psychiatrists can attest to the fact that far more time must be spent dealing with the difficulties accumulated by the chronically depressed person because of the depression than with the origins of the depression itself.

What are, in fact, complications of chronic depression are frequently experienced by people as miscellaneous problems that seem to have sprouted out of nowhere. Millions of men and women worry about their sex lives but are unaware of the subtle interplay between mood and sex. Marital conflicts often stem from communication difficulties caused by unrecognized depression and can become painful enough to bring husband and wife to the verge of divorce. Depression commonly disrupts communication. Because the depressed person is hypersensitive, he may misconstrue silence, for instance, as rejection and a lack of love. Because he is withdrawn, he may himself be misunderstood as rejecting others. He feels alone. "Wouldn't we all do better," he may think, echoing the journalist in Graham Greene's novel *The Quiet American*, "not trying to understand, accepting the fact that no human being will ever understand another, not a wife a husband, a lover a mistress, nor a parent a child? Perhaps that's why men have invented God, a being capable of understanding."

One situation in which chronic depression can be advantageous—and then only if it is correctly recognized and dealt with—is when the persistent mood serves as a *warning* to the person, telling him that there is something of a recurrent or ongoing nature in his home or work environment that is continually undermining his self-esteem. A woman married to a man who is ready to criticize her at the least provocation and is unappreciative of her contributions to family life; the vice-president of a company whose president is shortsighted, exploitative, and untrustworthy; the adolescent son or daughter of parents who are blindly arbitrary—any one of these individuals may be chronically depressed as long as he or she remains in the present environment and accepts such deprecation, however passively or unconsciously, without trying to correct the imbalance.

Why do certain individuals become chronically depressed rather than dealing with stress in an open and direct way through acute depression? The acutely depressed person is usually one who is in better touch with his emotions and feelings on a day-to-day basis, and who has learned ways of expressing them more effectively. The chronically depressed person does not have this ability. The acutely depressed person is more flexible, hence less likely to get trapped in his depressed mood. There may also be important biochemical factors that determine whether or not a depressive reaction will be resolved within a reasonable period or go on to become chronic. Studies of the neurophysiological operations of the brain point up the tendency of the depressed person to show alterations in the metabolism of the substances called biogenic amines, that affect the transmission of impulses within the nervous system. Other studies demonstrate that depressed patients show changes in the metabolism of hormones and of minerals such as calcium that are reversed only after the depression lifts.

Regardless of whether a person becomes acutely or chronically depressed, however, depression is still preferable to other ways of reacting to stress, such as psychosomatic disorders. As the person works his way out of depression, whether on his own or by means of newer approaches to psychotherapy combined, when appropriate, with new antidepressant drugs, he is also gaining the insight essential to strengthening his ability to cope with his future.

By contrast, psychosomatic illnesses—another form of stress reaction—carry with them a poorer outlook for recovery. Stress is known to be a major contributant to the development of cardiovascular disease, such as hypertension, as well as asthma, colitis, peptic ulcers, and other conditions. To have a heart attack or an ulcer is socially acceptable; it shows, somehow, that one has been a hard-working, success-oriented kind of person. Even though his health forces such a person to slow down, this is considered reasonable inasmuch as it is required for his physical well-being. It is not socially acceptable to be depressed.

And yet, whereas depression is nearly always completely reversible, the patient who has taken the heart attack or ulcer route for coping with stress must face the fact that these illnesses often leave in their wake physical damage that is irreversible. The ulcer patient, reacting to stress through psychosomatic symptoms, can bleed to death suddenly or end up either with a hole in his stomach or, through surgery, with no stomach at all. Still, the majority of men and women would, if asked, unwittingly prefer a physical illness to a depression. This widespread attitude encourages millions to avoid facing depression in themselves and doing something about it.

During the Presidential campaign of 1972 the public was stunned by the revelation that the Democratic Vice-Presidential candidate had been treated for depression—not just that he had been depressed, but that he had received medical attention for his depression. In spite of the fact that he had recovered and resumed his Senatorial responsibilities, Thomas Eagleton was forced—not because of his qualifications or character, but because of his medical history—to resign his candidacy. Any psychiatrist who has worked with patients who occupy positions of responsibility in government, industry, or education knows how fearful they can be that the depression from which they almost inevitably recover might become common knowledge among their associates.

Such instances reveal the extent of the average person's misinformation and fear regarding depression. In its own way it is more confusing to us and more disorienting than the Watergate scandals, which revealed lack of morality, contempt for human dignity, singularly poor judgment. But corruption in high places is an understandable and familiar phenomenon; depression is not.

It is time that we recognize the ubiquity and contagiousness of depression—as much a public-health problem as yellow fever or smallpox in their time—and realize that depression is not only a highly common way of reacting to stress, a reaction that sometimes requires medical attention, but that, when acknowledged, it is also for millions a unique opportunity to redefine themselves and resolve long-standing destructive conflicts within themselves and their environment.

2
An
Opportunity
for
Change

MOST OF US are well defended against knowing ourselves. As T. S. Eliot wrote in *The Cocktail Party*,

> Most of the time we take ourselves for granted,
> As we have to, and live on a little knowledge
> About ourselves as we were. . . .

Any event or any change in a person's life that forces him to break down some of these defenses, for whatever reason, is going to be painful. To experience acute depression is an opportunity for a person not just to learn more about himself, but to become more whole than he was.

Not only does depression afford a chance for insight, but "falling apart" can accelerate the process of reordering one's life after a serious stress—a loss, for

27

example. Becoming depressed is an inevitable concomitant of letting go—of a person, a position, a piece of oneself. The greater the attachment, the more involved it is with one's self-esteem and dependency needs, the greater the reaction will be.

The most common situation in which depression accompanies such a letting go is the reaction to the death of a loved one, or the breaking up of a relationship in which intense love has been involved. Freud, in his monograph "Mourning and Melancholia," attempted to distinguish between such grief reactions and depression. According to him, when a loved one is lost the normal response is grief, the abnormal response is depression. The difference was conceived of as being rooted in the kind of relationship that had previously existed between the two people, in particular whether there was any unconscious hostility and guilt toward the one who had died.

This distinction has proved misleading. It is much more useful to think of grief as being a form of acute depression, which becomes a more complicated problem when the person is so sensitive to the loss, or the loss is of such a nature, that he cannot manage the intense feelings without professional help. Far more serious is an inability to experience the depression at the time of the loss. The failure to become depressed drives the reaction underground, where it can silently exert its influence over the person's life for some time to come.

Our culture discourages the experiencing and expression of feeling. The individual is expected to conceal his emotions, often even from himself. No matter what the nature of the stress, he is expected to continue functioning efficiently unless he is physically unwell. Hence the preference for such somatic manifestations of stress as cardiovascular disease or intestinal disorders, which permit the person to become dependent and more or less incapacitated without embarrassment or censure.

Yet it is precisely the person who cannot respond with emotional pain when confronted with a significant loss who later becomes subtly and seriously compromised by chronic depression, frequently masked by physical ailments. When the situation warrants it, when letting go is a necessity, it is much better simply to break down. Acute depression affords such an opportunity.

Allen Stark was forty when his father died suddenly of a heart attack. As the shock waned, he found himself wanting to be alone, waking in the night, remembering, crying. His wife, who had always considered Allen the epitome of stability, was frightened by the openness of his feelings. As weeks passed, she became increasingly critical of him. "Haven't you cried enough?" she insisted, to which Allen replied: "How much is enough?"

How much is enough?

It took Allen nearly six months to recover fully from the impact of his father's death. During that time he experienced repeated episodes of acute depression. Tension and sadness would recur and last from a few hours to several days. At these times he found it difficult to concentrate and to communicate with his friends and family. Wondering whether his wife might be right, feeling embarrassed by the persistence of his grief, he spoke with his minister. After a few talks, he was reassured that his depressive feelings were quite normal. Through these discussions he was able to free himself from feelings of guilt and inadequacy, realizing that his wife's inability to understand his mood stemmed from her own fear of emotionalism. Once aware of this interaction, he could accept his own feelings in a sensible way and work through with his wife her tendency to see any show of emotion as "weak."

In addition, he reconsidered the nature of his relationship to his father, what his father had really been like, what his strong points were, and in what ways his father had been a disappointment to him. He thought carefully about what it meant to be a father himself. He felt a gradual lifting of his sadness and ultimately described himself as being "better put together than I was before."

In a changing society such as ours, in which alterations occur rapidly and often without warning, the opportunities for loss are especially commonplace. Psychiatrists who have studied the effect of culture on various emotional states have observed that overt depression occurs more frequently in tightly knit and highly organized societies, where the value systems are readily identifiable and the ways and means of avoiding depression are few and far between. Their studies also show that a society in flux is characterized by an extremely high incidence of hidden depression because of the great confusion in value systems—to the extent that one hardly knows where to draw measures for self-esteem—and the innumerable environmental changes encountered by the individual in relatively short periods of time. The depression is often hidden because in such a loosely structured society, the individual has many options for reacting to life stresses other than by becoming depressed—options that range from indulging in antisocial behavior to becoming dependent on drugs or alcohol to resolving problems in communication simply by terminating the relationship, as in divorce.

Change of any type, if it involves something or someone of importance to the individual, is usually a catalyst for depression. The process of growing up and growing older involves a series of changes; every transitional phase of life, from childhood to marriage to old age, requires some degree of giving up, of letting go. In order to move successfully from one phase to the next, a person must be able to experience depression in a direct and meaningful way.

Children can be depressed; when they are, the mood change is likely to show up primarily in their behavior. The beginning of adolescence is when the individual first becomes truly conscious of the nature of his inner emotional life and can recognize and feel depression as such. It is common for the adolescent to be depressed. He is experiencing himself for the first time as an individual and determining his impact on, and relationship with, other people. It is a period of separation for him, the first real separation between him and his parents. The fourteen-year-old begins to feel a need to break away, to be alone, to be with others his age. Nonetheless, he has a continuing attachment to his family and feels varying degrees of guilt about his apparent rejection of them.

Today's world is a particularly difficult one for the adolescent. Psychiatrist Peter Blos has described the adolescent as the pulse of society. If teen-agers are in a state of confusion and turmoil, they reflect a society which, analogously, is disturbed and out of touch with itself. The contemporary climate in America makes it especially difficult for adolescents to acknowledge and deal with being depressed. Faced with a multiplicity of standards, many have become bewildered, disenchanted, seduced into quieting their distress with sex, drugs, alcohol, apathy. The adolescent who at times experiences overt depression is not a problem to himself or society. Problems are created by the ones who cannot tolerate sadness or disappointment, who are out of touch with their emotions and have little understanding of what is happening to them. These are the ones likely to submerge their depression and replace it with such self-defeating behavior as dropping out of school or getting caught in an unwanted pregnancy.

Getting married is another example of a major transition likely to bring on depression. Marriage, regardless of how long the couple may have known each other before, and even if they have lived together for a time, requires major alterations in attitude and a reassessment in expectations. It is no longer just a man and a woman in love with each other or sharing each other's companionship. In addition to the details of living together in new roles, there is also the necessity of coping with friends and relatives in a new context. Economic considerations change. It is not surprising, therefore, that some degree of acute depression accompanies the giving up of the old freedom—even if such freedom only involved keeping one foot out of the door—and the initiation of a new and more permanent kind of commitment. When an acute depressive mood is unexpected and misinterpreted, or, as the family physician can readily support, disguised by the appearance of various psychosomatic problems such as headaches, urinary tract disorders, or fatigue, it can start to undermine the very core of the new relationship.

Becoming aware of, and making an effort to change, a pattern of behavior that has been self-defeating will often bring on an acute form of depression. Frequently, the behavior pattern itself reflects an underlying and unrecognized chronic depression. How the acute reaction may alert the person to his predicament and force him to deal with it is illustrated in the case of Robert Duncan, a fifty-year-old engineer, married for twenty years, who became acutely depressed. Three years before this mood change, several disturbing events had occurred. His mother had died. The company for which he worked had lost several government contracts, and as a result he had been laid off.

With several former associates, he had set up his own consulting firm, which struggled for existence in a poor economic climate. Not wanting to upset his wife, he concealed from her the extent of their financial crisis. When it came time to meet certain personal expenses, such as school tuition for their two children, he borrowed money, telling her that his new venture was growing.

He was under a great deal of pressure to make his new firm solvent. At the same time he did not sleep well, awakening at three in the morning anxious and worried. He put off making calls on prospective clients. His paper work fell behind. Meanwhile, he was rapidly constructing a web of deception with his wife in order to maintain his self-esteem in her eyes.

Suddenly his system collapsed. The banks from which he had borrowed demanded immediate payment of his loans. He could no longer hide the situation from his wife. She was, of course, shaken by his confession. For several days afterward he thought of suicide. "I can't face her again. She'll never trust me," he thought. His self-defeating behavior, which had dated back to his mother's death and his dismissal, was interrupted by events that set off an acute and painful depression.

He confided his desperation to a close friend, who suggested psychiatric counseling. Reluctantly he decided to visit a psychiatrist, who started him on antidepressants and proceeded to explore with him the important issues relevant to his depression. He had been hurt and angered by his dismissal, but could not deal with these feelings because they had been largely blocked out. He also felt guilty about losing the job, as if it had been a personal failure. His insecurity had caused him to fear that his wife would lose respect for him, so he fell back on a series of lies to hide his problems from her. While part of him was trying to make his new firm work, another part was working against him to undermine his efforts.

After six weeks of therapy he felt much better. He and his wife then had several joint sessions with the psychiatrist, in which they were able to renew communication and set a basis for the restoration of trust. Robert Duncan was not only relieved to have the facts out in the open, but he was also sleeping well, more energetic, free from his tendency to worry and put things off. He was surprised by the increase in his productivity. As he began to cope more aggressively with business matters, he and his associates obtained several important contracts that assured their survival as a firm.

Robert Duncan had approached professional treatment gingerly, partly because he still assumed that psychotherapy was indistinguishable from psychoanalysis—that it would take three years and fifteen thousand dollars to help him—and partly because he was skeptical of its value. "What can therapy do for me when my problems are real?" he thought. "Therapy can't get us contracts or restore my wife's respect for me." With the aid of therapy, and the disappearance of his depression, he was able to accomplish both these aims.

Acute depression, then, is a genuine opportunity to settle long-standing, unrecognized depression that has been operating in a subversive way for years.

One fifty-five-year-old woman came to terms with her chronic depression only when she became acutely depressed after her daughter developed severe rheumatoid arthritis. Until then she would never have considered herself depressed. Her hypersensitivity, her poor sexual adjustment, and her tendency toward social isolation had been viewed by her and her family as "personality traits" rather than signs of an underlying depression. She was just another human being subject to the usual stresses and strains of life, whose frustrations could best be handled by avoiding conflict and taking a drink or two when things became too rough. Her daughter's illness, which triggered an acute depression and forced her to seek counseling, gave her the very first realization of the way her chronic mood had been depriving her of a fuller life.

Finally, there is another, more complex function that acute depressive episodes serve. They can provide the individual with an opportunity to become more of a person, more sensitive, more creative, more effective after the depression has lifted.

Depression reduces vitality. The mood makes it difficult, if not impossible, to envision solutions to problems. Yet the majority of creative people, whether the term "creativity" is used in the narrow, artistic sense or in the broader sense of being able to see things in a fresh way and to combine concepts in an original manner, will attest to the fact that they have experienced significant episodes of acute depression from which they have rebounded to reach new levels of creativity.

Why is this so? Why would a period of being depressed and feeling hopeless be a prelude to a heightening in creativity? The answer lies in the nature of creativity itself. To be creative in any sense, a person must be able to relinquish old and fixed assumptions that block a fresh appraisal of a situation. Ten years ago, for example, it was assumed that a woman's femininity was contingent on an early marriage and having several children. More recently, there has been a fixed assumption that women will pursue graduate studies and/or a career even if this means the exclusion of marriage and family life. In either case, there is immense pressure on young women to conform to the particular bias that is in vogue.

The inability to be free from such influences cripples many young women in making decisions about their future, preventing them from using their imaginations and their knowledge of themselves to create the particular kind of life for which they would be best suited.

Pavlov and B. F. Skinner pointed out that the human being is inevitably conditioned by his family and society along a variety of lines. Such conditioning helps form an integrated personality structure. At the same time, however, many irrelevant, archaic, and even destructive patterns can become ingrained. The more rigid and intense the conditioning, especially when the individual is also insecure, the more unbending the personality. The more inflexible the personality, the less resilience and imagination he has to adapt to new or unexpected situations. Acute depression is a necessary vehicle for releasing a person from the bondage of such conditioning and freeing the vital elements of creativity. This phenomenon is regularly seen in the course of psychotherapy, where episodes of depression are followed by insight and greater flexibility.

Arthur Koestler, in his *Act of Creation*, refers to psychotherapy as an artificially induced regeneration relying on the basic process of *reculer pour mieux sauter*—to take a step backward in order to make a better leap forward. Koestler writes: "We found this pattern repeated on the level of human creativity: the scientist, faced by a perplexing situation—Kepler's discrepant eight minutes' arc, Einstein's light-traveller paradox—must plunge into a 'dark night of the soul' before he can reemerge into the light. The history of the sciences and arts is a tale of recurrent crises, of traumatic challenges, which entail a temporary disintegration of the traditional forms of reasoning and perception . . . [and] a new innocence of the eye; followed by the liberation from restraint of creative potentials, and their reintegration in a new synthesis."

3
The
Common
Traps

"I'M THIRTY-THREE YEARS OLD, and as far as I'm concerned it's over," remarked Walter Bergman. "Married to a woman who finds any excuse not to sleep with me. Doing a job I hate, way below my level of competence. The only thing I really enjoy is being with my kids. I'm caught in a trap."

Walter Bergman was depressed. He had been able to manage an ungratifying life situation for nearly three years until, one morning, after weeks of tiredness and irritability, he telephoned his superior at work and impulsively quit. The previous day he had been reprimanded for a minor error in his preparation of some sales information. In the ensuing weeks he became increasingly withdrawn, silent, and sulky. His wife insisted that she would have to leave him if he didn't see a psychiatrist.

Insidiously and with relentless precision Walter had constructed a complex trap, tailor-made for himself, which had finally emptied his life of meaning. Talented, one of the best students in his class at Yale, he had imprudently changed his career direction three times in ten years. First he flunked out of his first year of law school by simply not studying. Then he worked for a bank for several years, but quit because he was "bored" and not getting ahead quickly enough. Finally, he quit his job with a fund-raising public relations group because he felt unappreciated. In each instance he placed the blame for his dissatisfaction on people and things outside of himself. Now, unemployed, his work trap had snapped tightly shut.

Not content with an occupational trap, Walter built a personal one as well. In spite of his strong need for warmth and support, he married a girl who was basically critical and undemonstrative. He had initially been attracted to her sharp, analytic mind and impressed by her high level of energy. He made what seemed to him a rational decision, but in the process denied obvious emotional needs that were not likely to be met in the relationship.

His career confusion and his poor choice of a wife were linked to a period of low self-esteem that had begun shortly after he had finished college. At that time he was very much in love with a girl who ultimately broke off the relationship, leaving him painfully hurt and rejected. Rather than becoming acutely depressed at this time, he rapidly suppressed these feelings, pretending to himself that it really didn't matter. Whereas he had originally thought of studying jour-

nalism and political science after graduation, he suddenly felt that this direction would not afford him
enough prestige or money. He decided on law and
applied to the law school at the University of Wisconsin,
where he was quickly accepted. In his social life, he
adopted an attitude that becoming too emotionally involved was a poor idea since it would only lead to hurt
feelings; he became aloof and inaccessible in his relationships with women.

The denial of his intrinsic career interests for the
sake of prestige and money, and the denial of his
emotional needs in order to defend himself against the
possible hurt of another rejection, were the first steps
in the building of Walter Bergman's trap.

Walter Bergman is the prototype of millions of
men and women who are busily constructing traps for
themselves, or who are on the verge of experiencing
the acute fear and hopelessness that sweep in on them
once they realize that the trap has snapped shut.

The building of traps often follows the same basic
blueprint. The individual fails to cope adequately with
a stress or a series of stresses. Instead of reacting to
them appropriately and working the issues through, he
denies the feelings, shuts them out of consciousness,
and conceals them through the formation of mechanisms designed to protect him against future hurt.
Rather than facing his own complicity in his career
problems, Walter Bergman projected the blame for his
difficulties onto his environment. By denying the importance of warmth and sex in his relationships with
women, he ended up marrying a woman who could
offer him neither.

For many people there is a compulsive quality operating in the formation of the trap. One of the more common trap situations is seen in the efforts of men and women to reproduce in their own marriages the kind of family life they knew when they were growing up. This occurs regardless of the attitudes which they may have had about their upbringing. For example: A young man is reared in a home in which his father is a strong and dominant figure while his mother is quiet, uninvolved, and somewhat withdrawn. He sees his mother as ineffectual and his father as unkind. He resolves never to find himself in a similar position and ends up marrying a woman who is strong and independent, only to discover himself engaged again and again in a power struggle for control. If he makes a different error in judgment, he may marry a woman who appears quite self-reliant, only to find out, within a few years, that she too, like his mother, lacks initiative and a healthy respect for herself.

In either instance, by attempting to go to the opposite pole or by inadvertently overlooking personality characteristics in his wife-to-be, he has succeeded in constructing a trap for himself that has its origins in the kind of relationship his parents had.

Another route the trap can take is through the use of the environment to reinforce and confirm inner conflicts and constrictions. As a result of an unusually repressive childhood and adolescence, for example, in which initiative and creativity were seldom encouraged and conformity was demanded, a young man may develop serious obstacles to his ability to mobilize his energy and direct his inherent aggression outward toward self-selected goals. At the same time, afraid of

his own urges toward independence and unable to release his emotions, he cannot respond promptly and appropriately to stressful situations. His adaptation to life
is generally passive, and he is readily controlled by
others.

Failing to select a life style in which his inherent
need for freedom and initiative could be fostered, he
chooses instead an environment that reinforces his low
self-esteem. He then projects onto that environment
the obstructions that had previously been internalized.
For example, he obtains a middle-management position with a large manufacturing concern, where his
decision-making authority is very narrow and he is
discouraged from introducing innovative concepts lest
he be ridiculed and criticized.

The real trap now confirms the inner trap. The
circle is closed. The options available to the person
become progressively more limited.

If and when some part of himself, through a shift
in equilibrium provoked by a particular stress situation,
becomes aware of the trap, he may begin, finally, to
hurt. Human beings have a strong tendency to reaffirm
inner constrictions and deprivations by building external traps, and then to live within them in unhappy
equilibrium until something sufficiently dramatic occurs to wake them up to their dilemma. In the process
of creating such traps, they choose the wrong people
to marry or have a love affair with. They place their
trust in friends and business associates who prove untrustworthy. They handle money with special irresponsibility and choose occupations replete with frustrations
and designed to block personal fulfillment.

Winifred Regan, at twenty-nine, was unmarried

and worked as a rewrite editor for a large weekly magazine. Although she had graduated *magna cum laude* from Mount Holyoke, she had always been haunted by a sense of inadequacy. "I don't really see any point in girls having careers," her father had maintained. "No man is good enough for you, Winifred," her mother pointed out repeatedly, but then added, "Don't be too aggressive or you'll never get a man."

Winifred herself felt that she was a good student, but had no special talents. "I don't have the energy to go on to graduate school. I really don't know what to do." In this mood she took the first job offered her after graduation, with the production department of the magazine for which she was still working seven years later. The nature of her work prevented her from introducing her own ideas into articles. Most of the time she was engaged in a glorified form of proofreading. She was paid a relatively meager salary that barely allowed her to meet her expenses.

Great demands were placed on her time, leaving her with little freedom or motivation to do any writing of her own. She was too demoralized to search actively for another position. She was caught in a trap that repeatedly reinforced her low self-esteem, feeding again and again the inner conflict that had created it in the first place.

Traps can be built just as easily—and effectively —by men and women who have collected all the external evidence of social and material success. Adam Barclay was born poor. His family lived in Detroit. His father was an unemployed alcoholic and his mother worked as a clerk-typist. Adam was an unusually bright student and won acclaim again and again for his academic achievements. He was awarded a scholarship to the Wharton School of Business, from which he was graduated at the top of his class. "Damn it," he said to himself, "I'm going to make a million dollars before I'm thirty." And he did.

With two other men he started a chain of quick-food restaurants that flourished in the latter part of the 1960s. He worked eleven hours a day and on week ends. He was asked to be on numerous boards and to involve himself in community activities, all of which he accepted. In fact, he could not say no, since each new offer brought with it a new occasion to associate with wealthy and prominent men and women in his community.

By the time he was thirty-seven, he began to lose interest in the various enterprises he had built. "I want out," he told his wife, Ruth, repeatedly, "but I don't know how to get out. There's no one else who can run things if I leave." Ruth, in turn, had begun to drink more and more, out of loneliness and a sense of social inadequacy. She had grown up with Adam in Detroit and had never felt comfortable with their new friends. She avoided the country club and important social occasions as often as she could.

They had two children. The eldest, a boy of eleven, was an underachiever in school. He was very bright, but because of a painfully low level of self-confidence and a generally apathetic attitude, he could barely pass his subjects.

Adam Barclay's house in suburban Westchester had become a trap, a solidly constructed one built by his own hands as he drove himself relentlessly on to accept every new opportunity that came along. What had begun as his determination "never to be poor like my parents" became a compulsive need to accumulate more wealth, more power, more recognition than ten men would need in a lifetime. Adam realized this—painfully—but had no idea what to do about it.

Traps are constructed, on the whole, by human beings who are chronically depressed or who lack inner freedom, who are not what the late psychologist Abraham Maslow called "self-actualizing." According to his concept, the healthy and mature adult should be capable of identifying and moving spontaneously toward goals which are in keeping with his value system, reflective of his personality needs, and at the same time attainable within the environment, even though such achievement usually involves overcoming obstacles. The late psychoanalyst Lawrence Kubie stated that the mature person in touch with his feelings and abilities can consider and choose among legitimate options and can move toward worthwhile objectives with a freedom unknown to the compulsive or phobic person. The latter must repeatedly exhaust himself using "will power" to overcome inner resistances and fears. Only a small segment of the adult population can be said to be self-actualizing. The rest of us are more vulnerable to the game of building traps.

This has literally become a civilization of traps. Millions of people feel that the roads to sexual fulfillment, self-esteem, work satisfaction, financial security, equal opportunity, personal dignity, and spiritual meaning are closed at every turn. They are, however, sharply aware of a social and economic mobility that seems to promise, somewhere, somehow, the fulfillment of these needs. A society undergoing rapid change is a society of people painfully aware of unfulfilled ambitions. The white upper-middle-class couple in Lake Forest, Illinois, may hurt as much because of a lack of sexual and emotional fulfillment in their marriage as does the black family in metropolitan Los Angeles because of neighborhood violence and limited economic and educational opportunities. Obviously, the nature of the deprivation is different in these two instances. The role of the environment in preserving the deprivation is different. Nonetheless, the upper-middle-class couple and the family in the ghetto are caught in similar traps—expanding expectations with few visible signs of fulfillment.

Becoming aware of living in a trap—whether it is imposed by the environment or created by one's own machinations—will induce an episode of acute depression. Awareness of the self-made trap is the first in a series of steps leading to insight, and is usually experienced as a realization of its external fabric—the job, the marriage, the social situation—which is seen as the main cause of the hopelessness and tension. "I've married the wrong woman"; or "My husband has changed; I can't live with him any longer"; or "I've been passed over for promotion twice, and there isn't going to be a third time."

The next step in the process of insight also involves acute depression as the individual realizes how effectively he has collaborated with his environment in constructing his trap.

"I had just gotten my accounting degree," said a thirty-eight-year-old man in therapy. "I didn't want to get married, but Susan pushed it. We didn't have enough money, so she agreed to work. Supporting us like that made me feel kind of put down, and she never let me forget it.

"When the children came, I was making enough in practice so that she could stay home. We had a nice house, a good social life, lots of friends. Sex was just O.K. What really made me tense was the way she could go after me when she was angry. She made me feel that it was always my fault whenever something went wrong.

"I remember once we were supposed to meet some friends at a restaurant. I showed up early and Carol and Jim were there on time. Forty-five minutes later Susan showed up, angry. 'Why have you kept me waiting?' she insisted. 'You told me it was the Steak House, not the Lobster Pit. Lucky I called home to find out what you told the baby sitter. The least you could do is apologize.' I know I told her the right place, but to this day I feel guilty.

"Somehow or other I really needed Susan, and she knew that I felt I'd fall apart or something without her. I never had a real mother. My parents were divorced when I was four, and my father brought me up with a housekeeper. Mother married someone else and I didn't see much of her.

"We've been married fifteen years now. Last summer I really got depressed—couldn't concentrate, had to take three weeks off from work, felt nearly suicidal. Somehow I pulled myself together and went on, but from then on I realized that I was caught in a trap with Susan. I can't get angry at her. I can't stand my ground when she goes after me. She goes after me like a truck. I guess if I divorced her that might solve something, but I don't even think I can do that. I need her too much.

"I've been pretty depressed again this year, but now I know it isn't just Susan beating on me. It's how I can't handle it . . . how I actually encourage it . . . why I married someone like Susan in the first place, someone I thought I could depend on for strength."

A third step in the process of escaping from the trap involves changing the environment—finding another job, getting a divorce, encouraging one's wife or husband to cooperate in a process of improving the relationship. At the same time, there must also be an inner reaching for freedom from the conflicts and constrictions that induced the creation of the trap in the first place and nurtured it over a period of years. Each aspect—physically getting out of the trap, changing the environment, or modifying behavioral and emotional patterns conducive to trap-building—inevitably involves the experiencing of acute depression. One of the most important reasons why so few people free themselves from inner or external traps is their natural—though unfortunate—reluctance to experience the pain of acute depression. Again and again the psychiatrist sees in his patients the acute depression they experience when attempting to interrupt an ingrained pattern of behavior that has been detrimental to their lives.

Acute depression, in other words, alerts the individual to the fact that he has become entrapped. It will be activated by any efforts he makes to escape his trap. It will be an inherent part of the process of changing his personality so as to be free from the need to construct new traps.

One of the most dangerous traps of all is the failure to recognize the presence of depression and respond accordingly to its message. Denial on the part of the individual is reinforced by social values that encourage resistance to insight. What are these values?

In certain sections of our culture, it is considered better to engage in empty sexual affairs, to exploit financially but within the limits of the law, and to pursue self-defeating forms of behavior as long as these do not directly involve suicide or physical injury to someone else than to spend a few sleepless nights contemplating with some measure of anguish who one is and what one's life is all about.

In our society, it is considered all right to use drugs such as alcohol, amphetamines, and barbiturates to dull emotional pain. Regardless of the overt efforts to control such drug misuse, the continued spread of the problem strongly indicates the presence of factors in society that covertly encourage the use of such methods to block awareness and avoid facing depression.

It is helpful to project, to place the blame on others—one of the more popular mechanisms used to avoid facing depression and gaining insight—especially to place it on someone close to you or on large, readily identifiable groups, such as blacks or whites, employers or employees, youths or adults, men or women, that can serve as targets. Denying one's own problems and placing the blame on someone else is not only a temporarily effective way of postponing depression; it can also be a brilliant device for obscuring the real issues and elaborating on the original trap.

Jean Carter was a forty-three-year-old divorcée who worked as an interior decorator for a department store in Kansas City, Kansas. For seven years she had lived alone with her two children, a boy now seventeen and a daughter fourteen. During the previous eleven years of her marriage to Roger, they had rarely engaged in disagreements. Their sexual adjustment had been quite unsatisfactory for her and for him as well, but they never discussed it. Silently, each blamed the other for lacking in affection. They made no efforts to explore or improve the relationship.

Together they had created an adequate social life and achieved a place in their community. They were financially secure. They were a successful American middle-class family. Suddenly Roger demanded a divorce. Jane was shocked. She started to feel acutely depressed. After a few sleepless nights, she discovered that a drink or two before bedtime would help ease her tension.

Three months after the divorce, Roger married his secretary. "We have a lot in common," he told a friend, "and what a sex life!" The marriage lasted eighteen months. Meanwhile, Jane drank steadily more as loneliness pressed in on her. She dated occasionally, and went to bed with a few men who would take her to dinner. When she became aware of some feelings of depression and disdain in regard to these experiences, she could suppress them rapidly with a few martinis before her date arrived. "I like my freedom. It's quite a surprise. Roger was a horror. I know that now."

When her son dropped out of his senior year in high school, she called Roger. "He's your son. Do something about it." But by now Roger was into his third marriage and busily working in Boston. "The kid hasn't been in touch with me in nearly a year," he thought. "Besides, it's his problem. Let him work it out. They're all dropping out nowadays."

Jane Carter and her family can be considered victims of the trap of denial. They avoided communicating with each other about sensitive issues during their marriage. When the trap finally closed, she handled her depression through drinking and her husband handled his by rapidly building new traps for himself. They would not permit themselves to acknowledge and understand the depression warranted by the situation. Had they done so, they might have recognized the nature of their dilemma earlier. With this insight they might have resolved their emotional and sexual impasses. Or they might have terminated their marriage more sensibly and sustained their parental relationship.

To acknowledge that one is depressed is the first step toward escaping an entrapment or freeing oneself from chronic depression. It is essential, therefore, to recognize the many forms in which depression can appear.

4
How
to
Recognize
Depression

MOST PEOPLE FIND IT DIFFICULT to acknowledge that they are depressed. Psychiatrist Stanley Lesse found in his studies an average time lag of three years between the event responsible for the person's depression and the point at which he recognized that he was experiencing a depression.

It seems easy to write off episodes of depression as part of the human condition. Most men, commented Thoreau, "lead lives of quiet desperation." "Man's life oscillates like a pendulum between boredom and sorrow," wrote Schopenhauer. Sartre and other existentialists have emphasized that the individual must go through an awareness of hopelessness, experiencing the emptiness and anguish of life, as part of becoming capable of determining his own future.

Depressive moods are often suppressed or blocked out because most people would like to sustain a feeling of euphoria as much of the time as possible. Thus depression, being painful, is frequently denied.

A lowering of mood may cause a general slowing up in the thinking and actions of the depressed person. This change is misleading; depression is, in fact, an intensely active process, and hence painful. Even though the depressed person may withdraw from social contacts and experience a greater or lesser degree of immobilization, this response is *the effect of* the depression rather than the cause. Beneath the surface, at times beyond the person's real awareness, is a highly turbulent mixture of fear and anguish. The right questions, the right remarks, can readily tap it. It is not surprising, then, that fatigue is a common symptom of depression. Hypervigilance of the nervous system can be exhausting. The last thing any depressed person needs is a central-nervous-system stimulant, such as an amphetamine.

Because this inner anguish can be intolerable at times, there is a natural tendency to seek temporary relief through the use of commonly available drugs, whether "ups," "downs," or alcohol. There is also a tendency to ward off depression by such "antidepressant" forms of behavior as overspending, sexual promiscuity, compulsive overworking—patterns that ultimately reinforce the underlying depressive conflicts. Since depression is itself a new stress to which a person will react, his response to it can take many forms, ranging from boredom and ennui to overwhelming panic.

Perhaps the most common ways of coping with depression are to be dimly aware of it, procrastinate about coming to terms with it, engage in formidable rationalizations, and deny the significance of its signs: "I can't get to sleep at night, and I wake up at four or five in the morning. That's why I'm tired and haven't any interest in what I'm doing. If I could sleep I'd feel a lot better. Depressed? Of course not."

Most of us fail to recognize depression because we do not know what signs to look for. There are certain basic changes associated with depression, not all of which are present in every case. No two people manifest each and every emotional and behavioral change at the same time or even in the same way.

First, depression is commonly associated with a sleep disturbance. Most depressed individuals will notice a disruption in sleep habits. It may take them longer to fall asleep. They tend to waken more often during the night and sleep more lightly. They are likely to be up well before their normal time for rising. Waking hours—before falling asleep and after awakening in the morning—are passed stewing over problems and pressures. Though unaware of it, they are often afraid of going to bed at night and find any excuse to stay up. They are equally afraid of facing the day that lies in front of them.

Anyone with a significant or a long-standing sleep disturbance should consider the possibility that he is depressed.

The second important sign of depression is a lowering in sexual drive and ability. This can be especially troublesome in our culture, which places much value on sexual athletics. Such a change may indicate that the conflicts giving rise to the depression are of a sexual nature; more often it reflects a general decrease in energy or a rechanneling of energy into an effort to cope with the lowered mood. A waning of sexual interest should always raise the question of depression.

Closely related to the decrease in sexual drive are a loss of appetite and the disappearance of normal enjoyment in eating. These in turn lead to a significant loss in weight. A person may not even be aware of the fact that he is eating less than usual until he finds that his clothes are a bit too large and that the scales show a weight loss of five or ten pounds.

Finally, there is the subjective experience of the depression—how the person perceives what he is feeling. "I hurt all over inside." "I feel like crying most of the time, but I can't." "I cry too easily; I can't control it." "I'm just plain unhappy." "I've lost interest in everything I used to care about." "I'm scared as hell." "I'm bored." "I can't make a decision." "I can't concentrate effectively." "I feel just hopeless."

For many, the mood of depression is experienced as a lack of self-confidence. There is a close link between mood and self-esteem. People who feel that they are "failures," "worthless," "ineffective," "undeserving" are often, in fact, depressed.

If the individual is aware of the issues that seem to have triggered the depression, he may tend to dwell on them ruminatively. "Mother died five months ago. I can't get her out of my mind." "I really feel boxed in at work, by the people under me and by my supervisors." "This marriage isn't going anywhere." "I'm so terribly lonely since the divorce." "Why the hell can't we communicate?"

The depressed person often has a feeling of urgency and of being trapped. He can see no solutions to his impasses. There is no way out. His mood ranges from apathy to despair.

Sleeplessness, a lowering in sexual drive, a decrease in appetite, a loss of self-esteem, and an inner mood change ranging from boredom to frank hopelessness —these are the basic signs of depression. It is as if the biological energy flow that normally reaches out from the person to his environment has been blocked, while the inner agitation and anguish churn around within his nervous system. Being preoccupied with his own distress, appearing on the surface to be self-centered, unresponsive to outside stimulation, apparently indifferent to the needs of others—it is easy to see why the depressed person may at first provoke sympathy, then impatience, anger, and finally outright rejection —the very thing he most fears—from those who live and work with him but do not understand what he is experiencing.

A special group of people fail to recognize that they are depressed because of a tendency to cope with the stress of being depressed through counterreactions. Instead of losing weight, they overeat. Instead of a waning of sexual interest, they seek out sexual experiences almost compulsively. Instead of insomnia, they oversleep, partly as a result of tiredness but largely as a way of withdrawing from an environment they find unbearable.

There are other changes that result from being

depressed and that can serve as important clues. Diffi-culty in making decisions that otherwise could be made with little effort, problems with concentration, and a marked tendency to put things off are common. The depressed person may find it more difficult to write and read, but this is often rationalized as a loss of interest. He procrastinates in making plans or commit-ments, delaying everything from arranging a week-end social schedule to rewiring a lamp to looking for a new job. This, too, is often rationalized: "I'd do it if I had more time"; or "I'm basically lazy."

There is usually a need to withdraw from contact with others, even in people who are normally gregari-ous and outgoing. This aversion toward social contacts is not really a desire to be alone; the depressed person is often painfully lonely and fears rejection. Instead, it reflects a fear of interpersonal contact, caused partly by the inner pain and the exquisite sensitivity to care-less or unkind remarks. It is also a result of the over-all reduction in the outward flow of energy and in his ability to give of himself to others.

Because of a change in the perception of time, events seem to occur more slowly. For the depressed person the Bergsonian concept of mutable time is a reality. The person may feel slowed up, regardless of inner agitation. Consequently, the resolution of issues which in fact may be only days or weeks away seems to him to be an interminable distance in the future. "There is no turning back, no going forward. I feel helpless. The hours and days drag by. I can't stand it," is the way one woman described her hopelessness.

A person's ability to piece together these various

subjective changes and to admit to himself that he is depressed is certainly sharper when the depression is acute, and particularly when the triggering events are easily identifiable. It is much more difficult to detect depression when it has settled into a long-standing pattern, even to the point of being confused with personality characteristics ("This is the way I am, negative, a pessimist"), and when the mood cannot be related to its causes. Therefore, in determining whether someone is depressed, it is important to go beyond the questions "How do I feel?" and "How has my behavior changed?" and consider, in addition, "Am I the kind of person who might become depressed?" and "What kind of environment am I living and working in?"

The person should ask himself: "Have I experienced anything in the last few years likely to set off a depression? Have I been rejected by someone I loved? Has anyone died? Has anything happened at work to threaten my self-esteem?"

There are certain events that should cause some degree of depression; for example, a major change in one's life situation, for better or worse—a promotion, a divorce, the death of a parent or child, leaving home in adolescence, retirement, loss of physical health, financial reverses, marrying, having a child. When the reaction to such events is prompt and appropriately intense, the depression, being acute, is not hard to detect. However, when it begins slowly and builds up over a number of months or years, the insidious immobilization, insomnia, fatigue, withdrawal, and unresponsiveness may be hard to link to the source of these symptoms, and hence harder to account for.

Martha Wrightson was sixty-one years old when her husband died. She had been very close to him during the thirty-three years of their marriage. They had no children. She worked as a secretary to the president of a large bottling plant and continued, after her husband's death, to live in the same apartment they had occupied during his lifetime.

He died in June. She found it hard to cry. She shared her grief with no one. Instead, she tried to lose herself in her work. During the late summer she took a two-week vacation, but, finding herself bored and restless at the seaside resort, she cut it short and returned to work. The following Christmas holidays were especially difficult. She was lonely, often waking at night and missing having her husband in bed next to her. During the fall and early winter she noticed a tiredness that grew progressively more intense and that she attributed to her age and the weather.

In the early part of February, a few days before the anniversary of her husband's birthday, she found it hard to get out of bed in the mornings. She was late to work several times, which was most unusual for this very punctual woman. On her job, she began putting things off more and more. On several occasions her normally pleasant but by now impatient employer responded with annoyance to her slowness and seeming lack of responsibility. Although she felt that she was "in the wrong," her feelings were deeply hurt by his criticism. One day she impulsively handed in her resignation.

Fortunately, it was not accepted. Instead, her employer insisted that she speak with her family doctor about her health. At first she was tempted to reject his suggestion as an intrusion into her personal life. At the same time she sensed his real concern and decided to follow his advice.

Her physician recognized that she was depressed. He started her on antidepressant drugs and arranged to see her twice a week for half an hour, during which time he encouraged her to review and release the feelings she had stored up about losing her husband. A piece of guilt emerged. She had not pressed her husband strongly enough, she thought, to get an annual physical examination. "Had I done so, his cancer might have been picked up sooner. He might still be alive."

Within four weeks she was cheerful and energetic again, though still experiencing mild bouts of fatigue, as if she had recovered from a long illness. She was again doing her usual fine job and enjoying it.

For Martha Wrightson the slow emergence of her depression—in this case an inadequately handled grief reaction—prevented her from dealing directly on an emotional level with her loss. She could not relate the disintegration in her performance to her husband's death and her reaction to it because of the long delay between the causal event and the surfacing of her depression. She had not even considered herself depressed until it was specifically pointed out to her by her doctor. She was amazed to discover that the release of her feelings and the relief afforded her by antidepressant medication could so quickly restore her normal spirits.

In assessing her vulnerability to depression, Martha Wrightson could have considered another important clue: the kind of person she was. The personality of the individual is highly relevant to whether he may become depressed under certain circumstances.

The susceptible person is vulnerable to loss. Studies clearly support the fact that if a person has experienced a significant loss during his formative years, such as the death of a parent or other important family member, the vulnerability to depression is heightened. The susceptible person is also conscientious, responsible, and has a high personal ethic. He is quick to feel guilt, whether warranted or not, whether conscious and acknowledged or not.

He may be ambitious and energetic when in normal spirits, and competitive as well.

In spite of a tendency to be self-absorbed, he does care about the feelings of others, sometimes too much so, and may be overly cautious lest he inadvertently hurt their feelings. He has a strong need to be liked and respected. He tends to find himself in deep and sometimes overwhelming involvements and very dependent on those he loves. He is inflexible and has difficulty in setting limits. He is highly sensitive to anything that would reduce his self-esteem in his own eyes or in the eyes of others. Being rejected is an especially painful experience for him. His need for self-control is strong, yet paradoxically he is often vulnerable to being controlled by others without always appreciating the fact. He also has a need to maintain control over his environment, as a way of handling insecurities and avoiding hurt, and may become quite frightened when such control is jeopardized.

He has difficulty managing his hostility. At times

he is not even aware of his own anger. It is difficult for him to mobilize his emotions in his own defense, even when this is justifiable and necessary. Patience, usually a virtue, is often his liability. Over a period of time, in a job or a marriage where his hostility is repeatedly provoked, whether openly or covertly, or in an environment in which the normal expression of anger is severely suppressed, he may find it hard to maintain his emotional equilibrium.

A further clue to the presence of depression is the quality of the interaction between the person and his environment. An important question to ask is: "What kind of psychological climate do I live in?" In certain homes a free expression of ideas and feelings is simply not tolerated; in others, angry, deprecatory, and vicious feelings are repeatedly voiced. In working with depressed patients, the therapist can often identify a lack of communication within the patient's family and a lack of respect for ordinary sensitivities.

Similarly, the environment of an organization can reinforce the motivation and the self-esteem of those in it; or, by contrast, it can sabotage them by encouraging political deviousness through destructive competitiveness, and by stifling open communication. The individual working in such a setting may have a hard time holding onto his identity. He may become insecure and afraid of assuming responsibility: "If it works and is profitable, the organization gets the credit. If it fails, the credit is all yours!" He may become immobilized in his efforts, withholding his comments, refusing to introduce new ideas, doing only what has to be done to maintain his position, and reinforcing the demoralizing atmosphere within the entire organization. Such homes and offices can be considered *depressogenic;* that is, likely to induce depression in most of their inhabitants.

Certain occupations also seem especially depressogenic—medicine, for instance. Physicians have the highest rate of suicide, divorce, and psychosomatic disorders of any single occupational group. Corporate executives represent another group with a high incidence of stress-related conditions, such as alcoholism, cardiovascular disease, and other types of psychosomatic disorders. These statistics strongly suggest the presence of underlying depression, unrecognized and undealt with.

Recognizing depression, therefore, involves four major questions:

1. Are you experiencing any one or more of the cardinal signs of depression?
2. Have any major changes, good or bad, taken place in your life over the last few years that might have set off a depression?
3. Are you the kind of person likely to be susceptible to depression?
4. What kind of environment do you live and work in?

Even after such a self-assessment, depression may sometimes be hard to detect because it is concealed behind the particular way in which each person reacts to any stress, including the stress of depression itself.

5

Camouflage

WHILE IT IS IMPORTANT to envision depression as a way of reacting to stress, it is equally important to realize that *depression is itself a stress* to which the individual inevitably reacts. A mild depression that transiently impairs concentration and encourages indecisiveness may be barely noticeable in some people. By contrast, in another type of personality the same degree of depression may be experienced as highly painful and irritating. In other words, it is often difficult to tell *how much* depression is present from the overt reaction of the individual, since different people will react differently to the same degree of depression.

One case in point is William Agess, a specialist on the New York Stock Exchange. He worked on the floor of the trading center, where he was constantly involved in rapid-fire bidding and had to follow closely the swings in prices of various securities. He was conscientious, ambitious, and perfectionistic.

As a result of domestic problems, he became slightly depressed. Unable to sleep for several nights, preoccupied with his wife's complaints about their life together, he found it more and more difficult to attend to his work. He became frightened that he might make an important error involving thousands of dollars. This fear reinforced his depression until finally, seriously immobilized, he had to ask for several weeks off.

During his absence from work, he began to fear that his firm would find someone else to take his place. He had hoped to be named a partner within a year or so. Now, feeling that this was less likely, he experienced a growing rage at himself for his "incompetence." His anxiety mounted to such a degree that he often paced aimlessly about his apartment, further frightening himself and his family.

What had begun, in this instance, as a minor depressive reaction rapidly evolved into a nightmare—not because of the intensity of the depression, but because of William Agess's rigidity and perfectionism. Having a compulsive need to perform at a high level of efficiency at all times, he reacted to depression with panic.

Panic, like depression, is itself a psychobiological reaction to stress. In some research studies there have been reports of an elevated level of corticosteroids—hormones formed in the adrenal glands in response to stress—circulating in the blood of patients hospitalized for severe depression. However, this elevation in steroids may not be related to the depression itself, but to the stress of being depressed, since the abnormally high level usually returns to normal during the first week or ten days of hospitalization, long before the depression itself has begun to lift. Such a biological change would indicate a lessening in the panic the patient had felt during whatever circumstances led to hospitalization.

How a person reacts to being depressed, therefore, depends very much on his personality and environment. Some people are conditioned to giving up; others tend to drive themselves on more and more relentlessly. Compare these two instances:

Alice Larvin was a junior in college when she first became depressed over her relationship with a boy friend who seemed considerably less interested in her than she was in him. She became increasingly apathetic about her schoolwork, putting off term papers, finding it difficult to concentrate in class discussions. Though normally an active participant, she was now silent and slightly morose. She began to cut classes and spent her time in her room, ruminating about her situation. Occasionally she thought of dying, but dismissed such thoughts quickly.

After a month or so of lethargic, apathetic behavior, she decided to drop out of college and go home. Her parents did not seriously object. With their help, she obtained a part-time job at the local library. She felt "unhappy" but was also convinced that there was little or nothing for her to do about her state. When former boy friends called her up, she avoided speaking with them and refused to make any dates.

Except for some boredom and discontent, and occasional bouts of diarrhea and intestinal cramps, she settled into her new routine for over a year. Alice, in the face of being mildly depressed, had given up.

By contrast, Simon Rank, the executive director of a research institute in biologic sciences, became depressed when he was faced with sudden stresses both in his professional career and in his marriage. He felt torn between concentrating on improving his home life and maintaining his heavy responsibilities at the institute, where he was threatened by conflicts with his board of directors.

Simon began to work ten hours a day, preparing reports, going over plans and budgets. Being somewhat slowed down, and having trouble paying attention to details, he attempted to compensate in time and effort for what he had lost in concentration and decisiveness. At home his wife complained increasingly about the amount of time he was spending at the office. The time they did spend together deteriorated into arguments, with Simon pleading with his wife for more patience and understanding of the pressures he was under.

He slept about four hours a night, skipped meals and lost eight pounds, and felt utterly exhausted. Nevertheless, the worse he felt the harder he pushed himself—until he could push no longer. Unable to resolve his depression, and at the same time unable to withdraw from the field even temporarily, he suddenly developed heart palpitations and chest pains that forced his family physician to hospitalize him for a careful checkup.

In attempting to cope with depression, one person

may become a "work-compulsive" and another may withdraw into indifference and apathy. The personality of the individual—how he usually responds to stress —will have a strong influence on the particular way he reacts to a change of mood.

One of the most common ways of reacting to depression is the activation of anxiety and tension. The prominence of such feelings can often totally camouflage the underlying depression. Anxiety is, essentially, a state of apprehension, nervousness, mild fear, uneasiness. If it has an irrational focus, it is called a phobia; common phobias include fear of heights, of enclosed places, of crowds. Anxiety is often "free floating," unattached to any object but readily zooming in on ordinary preoccupations that concern everyone, such as financial difficulties or health problems. "If only I had a little more money, I wouldn't have any more problems." "Could this little lump in my breast be malignant? Maybe the doctor is wrong."

Anxiety is often associated with physical symptoms as well—heart palpitations, profuse sweating, dizziness, and weakness. It is physically distinct from tension, which involves a generalized tautness in the skeletal musculature of the entire body. People with severe tension often say that they feel as if they are in a "vise," a suit of armor that is too tight and that presses in on them. Tension, of course, may also be localized and involve only parts of the body, causing neck stiffness, chest pains, difficulty in breathing, headaches, or a tightness and heaviness in the muscles of the legs.

Whereas anxiety is caused by the person's awareness that something is wrong without his quite knowing where the danger is coming from, tension is usually caused by a recurrence of stress situations requiring that the individual cope by maintaining control over his emotions and the situation simultaneously. A salesman, for instance, confronted with a series of potential customers who are both rude and demanding, may have to resist the urge to flail out at them in a temper, thereby building up tension during that particular day. A highly conscientious computer technician may build up tension when his machine keeps delivering erroneous information and he cannot rapidly locate the error in the program.

Anxiety and tension are common ways of reacting to stress. When the stress is depression itself, they may become pronounced. Unfortunately, if the depressed person consults a physician, he is often treated only for anxiety and tension, and the underlying depression may remain camouflaged for a long time. A depression should always be suspected if episodes of anxiety and tension persist month after month, and are not relieved by such ordinary measures as recreation or a vacation and do not respond to tranquilizers taken on the advice of a physician.

If an individual has any psychoneurotic anxiety symptoms—and most people have some, such as mild phobias—he may respond to becoming depressed by a sudden upsurge in his fears.

At the age of twenty-three, Edna Markey consulted a psychiatrist because of severe phobias that clustered around traveling. She was afraid to ride in cars, trains, planes, buses. These constrictions had begun to develop in the course of her first sexual experience with a young man about whom she felt quite uncertain. When she terminated this relationship and gained insight through therapy into the guilt and ambivalence she felt toward sex and men, her fears subsided. She subsequently married, had three children, and lived a quiet, uncomplicated life. Although she never fully lost her fear of traveling, she was able, with the help of her husband, who did the driving, and by taking a drink or a tranquilizer before boarding planes, to get about quite well.

When she was forty-three, her mother died of cancer. At the same time, her eighteen-year-old daughter became pregnant and had an abortion. Edna herself was then about twenty pounds overweight and feeling somewhat old and unattractive.

Her husband, wanting to cheer her up after the funeral and her daughter's abortion, arranged for a trip to the Caribbean. She was pleased. But, as the day of departure approached, her fear of flying reached near-panic proportions. She insisted that the trip be canceled. Angrily, her husband complied.

Gradually, over the next few weeks, her fears expanded. At first she would not go anywhere in the car. Then she would not even leave her house. Any attempt to do so caused her to feel faint, frightened, tense. As long as she remained at home she was comfortable, although she did not sleep well at night. These fears forced her, of course, to avoid social engagements, and she was even unable to bring herself to attend her son's graduation from high school. Her family, having no understanding of what was happening, grew increasingly impatient with her behavior. This impatience, in turn, only reinforced her sense of hopelessness.

Edna Markey's traditional way of handling conflict and stress was to employ a mechanism known as dissociation; that is, to shut out of consciousness the conflicts she encountered and the feelings associated with those conflicts, and to develop in their place a net of phobic fears. This is a common maneuver employed by men and women with what is termed a hysterical psychoneurotic pattern of reaction. Naturally, when she became depressed, she reverted to her usual way of managing stress.

However, the clues to what she was experiencing could be found by looking at her behavior and for the moment ignoring her phobias that camouflaged the depression. She was immobilized and felt a growing sense of futility that she blamed on her immobilization. She slept poorly. She withdrew. All the elements of a depression were visible, but were unrecognized by either Edna or her family. Even the precipitating event, her mother's death, followed the classic pattern—the loss of a person important to her.

Depression, then, is a reaction to stress that itself becomes a stress and is handled through the particular mode of behavior characteristic of each person. For certain people it is vitally important to function at a high level of effectiveness, and the slowing up and constriction ordinarily associated with being depressed represent a special threat to them. Others tend to overeat under pressure and, when depressed, will show a marked increase in weight, rather than a loss, as they fill up with food to relieve their sense of emptiness. For some, direct physical tension is the primary way of acknowledging the change in mood.

Whenever Harold Vetter was under pressure, in

business or in his personal life, he could "feel it." The muscles on the back of his neck were tight. He felt a tautness in his calves, and would often play squash or walk a couple of miles to loosen up. Because of chest pains every now and then, he was afraid that he might be having a heart attack, and he was reassured only when an electrocardiogram showed that his heart was normal. From time to time he developed headaches, but aspirin would usually relieve them. "I'm a tense guy. When you're involved in the textile business—a hell of a lot of risk and one uncertainty after another, tough, competitive—you're going to get tense. A lot. But I've figured out ways to beat it. They always work."

When Harold became depressed after his only son's failure to obtain admission to law school and Harold's discovery, a few months later, that his wife had been having an affair, he did not recognize his depression as such. He felt no despair; and though he was resentful, he felt no more pessimistic about life than usual. Moving out of his home to a small apartment, he continued to play golf on week ends, occasionally took out models and buyers, and began to show up for work at six thirty in the morning.

Now, however, his ordinary methods for releasing tension began to fail. Tension kept him awake at night. His headaches increased in frequency and duration, and aspirin barely touched them. After a game of squash he felt tighter and more fatigued than he had in the past. At work, the ordinary pressures in his everyday life now affected him profoundly. Being tense, he was frequently sharp and angry with his partners and employees. He felt as if his body were constantly in a

strait jacket, which sometimes closed tighter and
tighter around him until he could hardly breathe.

Harold saw his doctor several times. The physician's reassurance about his physical health was no
longer enough to quiet his fears, and during his last
visit he stormed angrily out of the office, shouting that
he would find himself another and more competent
doctor. When his wife's lawyers attempted to initiate
a reconciliation, he made it clear that he was not about
to go home again, nor would he give her a divorce.

At no time did it occur to him that he was depressed. Tension, irritability, and concern about his
physical health combined with his conviction that the
"world was against him" to deprive him of the insight
that he was reacting, true to his form, to the stress of
being depressed.

Attempts to reduce tension or anxiety that
conceal depression usually fail, whether such attempts
take the form of a vacation, a divorce, or a change of
jobs, since the real mood change remains unrecognized
and unresolved. Because depression can manifest itself
in so many different ways, the average person may
be confused over what he is experiencing. At times he
must echo Steve McQueen's question at the end of the
film *The Sand Pebbles*. After performing a series of
daredevil feats and, at last, finding Candice Bergen to
love, McQueen is killed in the final two minutes of
the movie, in contrast to the usual ending of such ad-
venture stories. His last line is: "What the hell happened?" Many people, as the reaction to the stress of
depression hits them, also wonder what the hell
happened.

Psychiatrist Norman Reider states: "With the

mention of the word 'depression,' a patient will acknowledge, 'Oh, yes! I am depressed.' Often a sense of
relief may occur when the patient is told that his sense
of fatigue and lack of energy are not due to anything
physiological. At last it all makes sense. He can now
understand that what he has been experiencing is a
depression." Existential psychoanalysts, such as Ludwig Binswanger, departing from the traditional psychoanalytic mold of seeking answers primarily in the
patient's history, have encouraged therapists to ask not
only what the patient is experiencing, but *how* he is
experiencing it.

This is a crucial question in the matter of depression. Many people will use the term "depression"
loosely, saying that they are depressed when in fact
they are not. And many, because of the way in which
they react to being depressed or because they are out
of contact with their inner feelings, will deny being
depressed when, in fact, they are.

"I'm not really depressed," stated a young woman
of twenty-eight. "I'm lonely. I'm so lonely that it hurts.
As long as I have a boy friend, I'm fine. I can be alone
then, and read or putter, and it doesn't bother me.

"But when I don't have anyone, I get so agitated
that I could jump out of my skin. I can't do a thing. I
can't bear being by myself."

"Frightened, I'd say," said a forty-year-old
woman. "I'm always afraid, of losing my husband to
another woman, of losing my job, of something terrible
happening to one of my children. These fears haunt
me. I haven't always been this way, only for the past
year, since we moved to our new house."

"Afraid of being a homosexual," answered a third-year medical student, "of being queer. Ever since last term, when we had our lecture on sexual abnormalities. It really troubles me. Sometimes the thoughts crowd in so much I can't concentrate on my work. I feel like quitting school for a while. I must really be in bad shape.

"I haven't had any homosexual experiences, of course. But I have had a hell of a lot of difficulty making it with girls I like."

"Angry," said the middle-aged social worker. "Angry at the whole goddamn world, day in and day out. Not bitter, you understand. Just angry."

"Empty. An emptiness that makes me want to die."

The existential analysts emphasize that the way in which a person describes what he is experiencing is an invaluable clue to the nature of the underlying problem. For instance, when Edna Markey, whose depression was manifested as a rash of phobias, was asked in therapy *how* she experienced her phobic condition, she replied: "It's crippling. I feel like a prisoner, as if I have been guilty of some crime. My husband and children are angry at me, and that makes me feel really worthless. I don't want to see my friends. I feel like a failure as a mother. Somehow, I feel it's my fault that my daughter had to have an abortion. If my mother were alive now, she'd feel it was my fault."

At once the depressive quality of Edna's experience and the enormous guilt contributing to her state are apparent when the "how" of what she is experiencing is explored, when one goes beyond the more visible manifestations of her reaction.

The case of Simon Rank is similar. "There's no

other way," he said, describing his compulsion to over-work. "I am convinced that if I stop moving, every-thing will fall apart. I won't be able to get started again. I have no choice. I can't be spontaneous any more. Life drives me, I don't drive it. I am really scared of being helpless. There isn't anyone to depend on. If I stop, I'm dead."

The complex ways in which people experience themselves make it difficult to measure "how much" depression may be present. Simon Rank, with his strong determination to keep his life in one piece, his en-ergetic attack on the world in the face of falling apart, may indeed have been quantitatively "more depressed" than Alice Larvin, who quit school, went home for a year, and gave up rather than push against obstacles built by depression. To the casual observer, Simon Rank's ability to cope might well conceal the depth of his despair, whereas Alice Larvin's compliance with her unhappiness might conceal the mildness of her depression.

Recognizing depression, therefore, is complicated by the fact that depression, being a shock to the human system, will be handled by each person in his or her own way—sometimes through acting out.

The psychiatrist uses the term "acting out" to de-scribe the translation of an inner conflict into a be-havioral change. Releasing anger in a direct way, for example, is not a form of acting out. By definition, acting out implies that the individual is not aware of how his action pattern is determined by his inner con-flict. Hence, until he gains insight it is beyond his con-trol. The depressed teen-ager who repeatedly provokes his parents and teachers by not studying and by defying rules is not likely to establish for himself the connection between his inner sense of hopelessness and the behavior which evokes, again and again, the disappointment of, or punishment from, his elders. The fifty-year-old man who is involved in an affair with a younger woman at work may not realize that his sexual and emotional arousal is protecting him against coming to grips with a fear of aging, and may indirectly reflect anger against his wife and family.

Alcohol and other drugs supply one of the most common methods of translating an inner conflict into a behavioral one, as a way of reacting to an unrecognized depression. Because alcohol enhances sociability (the depressed individual often has to work against his tendency to withdraw from social contacts), dulls the emotions, decreases inhibitions and permits the liberation of anger (which the depressed person finds difficult to cope with), and promotes the further suppression of the idea that there is anything wrong, it is a temporarily effective way of blocking out the painful feelings of being depressed.

But it is a double-edged maneuver. Alcohol is, in fact, a central-nervous-system depressant that will ultimately intensify the underlying depression. "I feel so rotten," one habituated drinker often complained, "I'd like to die," and then, taking a drink to feel better, he inevitably felt worse.

To be habituated means to be dependent on the particular drug, in this case alcohol, or on the behavior pattern, such as promiscuity, as a way of coping with stress. Addiction is another matter. The person who is

addicted to alcohol experiences a biochemical change
—the nature of which is not fully understood—so that
his body requires the continued use of alcohol in order
to feel comfortable and meet certain physical demands.
Addiction is the result of the interaction between the
alcohol and the cells of the central nervous system.
Once it has taken place, it is irreversible. All heavy
drinkers are not addicted, but for those who are, a
single drink is enough to activate the underlying chemical process of craving.

Alcoholism is only one of a number of drug routes
for escaping a confrontation with depression. Insomnia,
a common sign of depression, is often combated with
barbiturates and other sleeping tablets used regularly
over a period of years, causing the person to lose confidence in his ability to fall asleep spontaneously and
inducing habituation and addiction. Other drugs that
affect behavior—amphetamines, marijuana, lysergic
acid diethylamide (LSD), and even heroin—are often
taken in an attempt to cope with unrecognized
depression.

A seventeen-year-old girl was brought to a psychiatrist by her parents because she had been using
alcohol, barbiturates, and amphetamines for over two
years. She attributed her drug usage to experimenta-
tion, but a careful review of her history revealed that
she had been depressed, without knowing it, ever since
her parents' divorce three years earlier. Shortly thereafter she had become pregnant and had had an abortion. Afterward she had started to feel some degree of
depression, which subsequently disappeared as soon as
she began using various drugs. Acting out is a common

phenomenon among teen-agers. It was not surprising, therefore, that she attempted to cope with her reaction to the disruption of her home through drugs and by becoming pregnant. The studies of psychiatrist Lawrence Downs show that many women whose pregnancies end in abortion have become pregnant to resolve—subconsciously—a problem in self-esteem caused by a period of depression.

The many different ways in which people react to depression may camouflage the depression itself, causing them to delay coming to terms with it. Behavioral disguises are the most blinding and the most likely to promote trap-building. In a culture characterized by a multiplicity of value systems and by a high degree of personal and geographical mobility, there is more than ever a trend toward translating depression into patterns of behavior rather than patterns of feeling— behavior that may occasionally be frankly antisocial, but that always and ultimately does harm to the individual who seeks in motion alone an escape from depression.

6
What
to
Expect
of
Psychotherapy

Too OFTEN, people who are aware of being depressed postpone seeking professional help because they don't know what therapy has to offer them. For many, psychotherapy is synonymous with a kind of cartoon conception of traditional psychoanalysis. In the film *Bob and Carol and Ted and Alice*, there is a brief scene between Alice and her psychoanalyst—the latter a caricature of the typical psychiatrist. Alice is desperately trying to express her ideas and feelings. He listens impassively as she struggles on, offering no particular assistance. Toward the end of the session she suddenly opens up, begins to communicate, to grasp insights about herself. At that point he looks at his watch and announces that he will see her the following Thursday. She is startled and wants to continue. He says only that he will see her the following week. In the film it is a hilarious moment. For millions it confirms the lurking suspicion that psychotherapy is a rather ineffectual and costly procedure, and that they have little choice but to go on living and battling with their unhappiness.

Since the depressed person already feels hopeless, it is not difficult to convince him that there is no resolution to his problems. And since he often sees his difficulties only in terms of his life situation, and not in terms of how he views and copes with it, he logically asks himself: What can a doctor or counselor do for me, anyway—find me a new job? change my wife's attitude toward me? balance my budget?

The psychiatric profession has itself contributed to this resistance by cultivating a philosophy of therapeutic exclusiveness. Therapeutic exclusiveness means, basically, that the therapist is familiar with one or two approaches to the resolution of emotional conflicts and tends to use his skills in a narrow way, without due reference to the patient's condition or particular set of problems. The traditional psychoanalyst psychoanalyzes his patient on a couch four or five times a week. The group therapist meets weekly, or for an encounter session on a long week end, with seven or eight participants, and focuses on interpersonal relationships or transactional analysis. The biologically oriented psychiatrist gives antidepressant drugs or electric convulsive treatments, often without much attention to the psychological components of the person's state. The primal-scream therapist waits for the patient's primal scream, and the gestalt therapist encourages him to punch a pillow as a substitute for his mother, whom he hates. Breathing exercises are used to reduce anxiety;

transcendental meditation is designed to reduce intellectualization and bring the individual in greater contact with sensory experiences, reducing tension in the process.

The diversity of therapeutic approaches makes it difficult for any single professional to be trained in depth in all the methods available. He could, if he abandoned therapeutic exclusiveness, be better able to understand the usefulness and limitations of the methods he has mastered and to know how to adapt them to the particular needs of various patients. He would also know when to call upon outside consultation or when to direct a patient elsewhere for therapy.

In recent years, psychiatrists have become increasingly oriented toward taking such an eclectic approach to treatment. However, the professional, not unlike everyone else, is profoundly affected by the popularity of a particular school of thought. Until the 1950s, traditional psychoanalysis was considered the cornerstone of treatment by many psychiatrists, and any other approaches to therapy, such as the cultural focus of Karen Horney or the psychobiological concepts of Adolph Meyer, were regarded as watered-down versions of the "real thing." With the advent in the mid-1950s of the tranquilizer chlorpromazine and in the early 1960s of the tricyclic antidepressants, the emphasis shifted to a more biochemical approach to the treatment of emotional disorders. By the late 1960s a major breaking away from long-term analysis and a reaction against the use of psychopharmacologic agents took place in the upsurge of interest in group therapy, encounter groups, and transactional analysis.

At the same time the psychiatrist was no longer

the primary therapist for those in need of emotional help. The psychologist, the social worker, the clergyman, the nurse, and the schoolteacher were recognized as vital members in the network of mental health services. Unfortunately, this advance was handicapped by the inherent tendency of the professional to compete with representatives of other professional groups, while competing with equal petulance with other members of his own group. What developed was not a team approach to the resolution of psychological ills, but rather, in most instances, one professional group vying with another for the right to treat, with an almost dogmatic insistence on the superiority of its own method.

As a result, while a number of people in distress sought the relief of a particular method that happened to be in vogue, the majority simply stayed home floundering, building bigger and better traps, becoming more convinced that given a choice between the absolutism of B. F. Skinner and the absolutism of Freud and the absolutism of Eric Berne, they might as well try to do it on their own. It cost less. They would not have to become exposed or dependent. And psychotherapy more or less smacked of charlatanism anyway. That the need remained was clearly reflected in the incredible sales of *I'm O.K., You're O.K.* and *Everything You Always Wanted to Know About Sex But Were Afraid to Ask.*

Most people felt that they were "not O.K.," particularly those immersed in chronic depression, which had lowered their self-esteem to begin with. Because they had little idea of what to expect of professional guidance, it could be said that the position selected was "I'm not O.K., but then neither are the professionals." This resistance to seeking help was reinforced by another important consideration as well; namely, that to reach out for guidance was to admit that one had failed, in a culture which insists upon success, and that to become a "patient" only confirmed the depressed person's low self-esteem. In the struggle to gain a sense of being "O.K.," it seemed important to stand on one's own two feet at all costs.

The decision to reach out for help is often half the battle. Consider the variety of ways in which people actually make the decision to consult a professional:

"I came to see you, doctor, because my wife said that she would leave me if I didn't."

"I've hit a plateau. I had some therapy years ago and it helped me a great deal. Recently I've noticed a loss of interest in my work and a kind of boredom with things. I'd like to see if I can get going again."

"I can't finish my term paper. A friend of mine said you might be able to give me some pills to help me get more energy."

"I really came to see you about my mother. But I've always had the idea of straightening out a few things in the back of my mind. I'd like to go on with some therapy for myself for a while."

"My parents told me to come. I don't want to. I don't see why I have to see a psychiatrist just because I smoked some pot and didn't pass my math and French."

"I want to leave my husband. I want you to see him so he doesn't fall apart."

"I asked my doctor for the name of a therapist. I know I'm depressed because I can't sleep at night and I can't concentrate on my writing. He was reluctant, wanted to give me pills, but I insisted."

"I didn't intend to commit suicide, doctor. I cut my wrists because the physical pain took away the hurting inside."

People consult psychiatrists because they have some insight into what they are experiencing—depression—and want professional help. They come at times because they are not getting what they want out of life. Often such circumstances as an angry husband or wife or an irate employer force them to come. Sometimes, by taking an overdose of barbiturates, they put themselves in a position of having little choice.

Because of the feeling of hopelessness inherent in depression, many do not expect to be helped. This negative attitude is often reinforced if they have already built a set of traps from which it seems difficult to extricate themselves. It is further aggravated if they see the problems primarily in terms of unchangeable external circumstances.

The first few contacts the person has with the therapist are critical in establishing a basis for recovery. The quality of these contacts depends largely on the experience and approach of the therapist. There are certain things he must do.

He must contribute to the establishment of rapport. So much has been written and said of transference—in which the patient projects onto the therapist fears and expectations that belong to earlier relationships with a parent, a sister, a friend, a lover—that not much has been said about the importance of rapport. Rapport is essentially a harmonious relationship that exists between two people, an interaction that permits the evolution of trust, communication, and sharing. The factors that give rise to good rapport, or poor rapport, are complex, but we have a few clues. The studies of psychiatrist Frederick Redlich and sociologist August Hollingshead indicate strongly that therapists are most effective when working with patients from similar cultural backgrounds and least effective when these backgrounds are grossly dissimilar. Paradoxically, the therapist with a very different background from his patient's will probably be much better able to write up the case and present it in a medical journal or at hospital rounds precisely because he cannot identify with the person and can maintain the doctor-patient separateness that contributes to a scientific understanding while, at the same time, interfering with empathy.

It is remarkable how seldom patients, in their early consultations, try to find out such relevant information as the experience, training, and approach of the therapist. There is a curious tendency to accept him on faith, and occasionally no attempt to evaluate, in direct contact with him, the kind of person he is. Many patients actually have continued for years in counseling and treatment situations with people they have intensely disliked, on the assumption that this was somehow irrelevant or might in fact be part of the treatment process.

For therapy to work, there must be a mutual trust and respect, a confidence and a liking, between the parties involved. Both therapist and patient must determine early on whether this is present or not. Rapport is the matrix of therapy, and only within this framework can what happens eventually happen at all.

As part of this rapport, the therapist should be able to empathize with the patient's feelings and predicament. Empathy is the ability to put yourself in someone else's shoes. The empathetic person understands what you are experiencing. In some way, he has experienced similar events or feelings himself. It is quite a different phenomenon from sympathy, which is to "feel sorry for." There are moments when it is appropriate to feel sorry for another person, as when the therapist listens to the patient relate how, in a single month, she lost her father, her husband, and her job. But it is not the therapist's sympathy that promotes her confidence. It is his empathy that encourages the patient to feel she is confiding in someone who will really understand. This quality in the therapist will lessen the patient's fear of further losing self-esteem by having entered therapy.

"I need you" is a difficult admission for many depressed patients to make, and the response of the therapist is a delicate one. Somehow he must be able to respond to this need without putting the patient down in the process. The position he cannot afford to take is "I'm the doctor, you're the patient, and that puts me one up." At the same time he must retain the authority that the patient has invested in him because of his professional role. The situation is not unlike that of the parent or teacher in dealing with adolescents; it is necessary at one and the same time to relate to them as individuals, on an equal and respecting basis, without completely relinquishing the authoritative role intrinsic to being a parent or a teacher.

From this authority base the therapist communicates, verbally and nonverbally: "I know what you are experiencing, and no matter how you regard yourself now, I can be of help in restoring your self-esteem and your ability to cope. I know you hurt, but hurting this way and coming here to do something about it are the beginning of a cure. I don't like to use the word 'sick.' It's misleading. It's much better to consider that there has been something wrong in your life or in your way of coping with life, and that now, finally, you have decided to do something to correct it. Most patients are a great deal better off after therapy than they were before they became depressed."

In these first few contacts, the therapist concentrates on acquiring data. Is the patient actually depressed? If so, when did the depression start and what seems to have triggered it? To what degree has the depressive immobilization interfered with his ability to function? What kind of person is the patient? What has been his life history—where did he go to school and what kind of marriage has he had? How many jobs has he held and how well did he do at these? Why did he change employers at various times? What losses has he experienced, what blows to his sense of self-worth? What does he think is the cause of his mood? How does his family regard him?

Often a patient will be confused as to the actual cause of the depression, particularly if it has been of long-standing duration. The very process of reviewing the facts provides a sense of coherence, and the establishment of rational links in the chain of emotional reactions helps reduce his fear of losing control.

In the traditional psychoanalytic process, and to a lesser degree in the nondirective approach to counseling advocated by Carl Rogers, the therapist allows the patient's story to evolve over a series of sessions without asking pertinent questions or helping him to understand it or to piece it together. "You haven't said anything to me," many patients complain. "Why don't you offer me some direction?" To which they receive the reply, "That's not the way therapy works." An extremely nondirective approach may be the method of choice in counseling certain individuals, but it is generally not well suited for the therapy of the depressed patient. It quadruples the amount of time required to get results. It denies access to important information simply because the patient does not realize its relevance. Most important, it encourages an already discouraged and often guilt-laden individual to project onto his therapist the anger and rejection that he expects to receive and that he feels, being "worthless," he deserves.

Silence, inappropriately used by the therapist in communicating with the depressed person, allows the depression to intensify and permits the patient to make many false assumptions. One patient described his experience with prolonged silences on the part of the therapist as follows: "He just sat there, staring at me. I felt uncomfortable. That's too mild a word—I was scared. I didn't know what to talk about. Besides, I felt slowed up, I couldn't concentrate very well, I found it hard to be spontaneous. So we both sat there for minutes that seemed endless.

"After a while I began to feel that he didn't really like me, that he disapproved of me. I asked him whether he did or didn't and he simply wouldn't comment at all. When I asked him whether he thought I should break off the affair I was having with this girl, he just replied, after a long pause, that it wasn't his place to make decisions for me. If I felt rejected before I started therapy, I really felt rejected after a few visits like that."

The depressed person should expect some participation on the part of the therapist, a participation that does not preclude listening and does not represent a rude thrust of the therapist's biases and opinions into the far reaches of his personal life. The therapist is not there to tell him what to do. Nor can he be expected to comment or point out issues and reactions before he has a sufficiently comprehensive understanding of the patient and his difficulties. What he can be expected to do is to initiate a certain amount of the exchange and to respond in an appropriate manner to the needs of the patient as they emerge.

One of the earliest needs the patient expresses is the desire to have some idea of the actual structure of the therapy itself. He usually has some preconceived notions as to what is going to be involved. He often assumes that he cannot afford either the time or the financial expense of therapy. "I couldn't possibly come three times a week for a year, as a friend of mine has been doing," said one patient, who was then surprised when he was told that one visit a week for a few months might well be all he would need. "How can you really help me without knowing my wife?" asked another patient, who was subsequently relieved when the therapist suggested having joint sessions.

When psychoanalysis was in vogue and the average analyst devoted forty hours a week to the therapy of eight analysands, it was not uncommon for the person making the referral to ask the analyst: "Can you take on a new patient or are you 'filled'?" Under such circumstances the individual, if accepted for the first visit, usually arrived expecting to be taken on as a patient. Still viewing the psychiatrist in the same way, many physicians and other colleagues, when calling him to ask whether he can "take on" a new case, expect a yes or no answer. A more appropriate reply would be: "It depends." It does depend on the nature of the problem. A consultation visit or two will give the psychiatrist a chance to evaluate the situation and decide, with the patient, what should be done.

Although the healing process begins from the moment the individual decides to do something to help himself, the first few visits must be considered consultative in nature. The therapist cannot possibly decide what course to take and what to recommend until he has had a chance to know the person and the problem.

There is still a sixty-minute hour and a fifty-minute hour. There is also a forty-five-minute hour and a thirty-minute hour and a fifteen-minute hour and a three-minute telephone call. There are still patients who come for psychotherapy three times a week for three years, but there are as many patients who come for a dozen visits over a three-month period.

The emphasis should be on flexibility. The patient should make as many visits as he requires to accomplish the particular goals of his therapy: relief from his depression, an understanding as to what caused it, modification of his methods of coping and his perception of himself so as to benefit as much as possible from his depression. An acute depressive reaction may be successfully managed in a few weeks. If the depression has been chronic, and particularly if in the context of chronic depression the patient has constructed a network of traps, therapy could easily extend over several years.

Together the therapist and the patient establish a structure and pattern to the therapy, based on the needs of the situation. Within this framework, of course, the patient should expect shifts and changes and modifications as therapy evolves. Such changes apply not only to the frequency and duration of visits, but also to the character of the patient-doctor relationship and the approaches or techniques the therapist uses in treatment.

Early on in therapy, the psychiatrist may withhold his own emotional reactions from the patient so that he can remain a somewhat neutral figure upon whom the patient can project and form transference experiences. As therapy progresses, however, the psychiatrist may reveal more of himself as a person, sharing his own feelings and reactions with the patient in the interest of the patient's insight. For instance, if a pattern of being late for interviews begins to stir up in the therapist a sense of impatience, since he never has enough time allowed him to pursue important areas for discussion, he may confront the patient with his behavior, and also with the frustration he himself feels as a result of the pattern. The chances are that the patient's tendency to procrastinate is provoking anger and rejection in other people as well, and this reaction on the part of the doctor may well afford the patient a direct opportunity to understand and change his self-defeating mode of behavior.

Depression affects how the patient thinks and feels in ways the therapist can usually anticipate. As a rule the patient's attention is focused largely on his depression and on the concerns that preoccupy him. "All I can think about," said a forty-one-year-old advertising executive, "is my loneliness. I keep going over and over again in my mind how my wife left me. I keep wanting to call her up and scream at her to come back." The term for the therapist's technique for dealing with such persistent feelings is "decentralization." Its purpose is to move the patient's attention away from his obsessive concern so that he can see what is happening with better perspective and, if necessary, more thoroughly let go of what he has already lost.

Equally common in the depressed person is a destructive preoccupation with what he *might* lose. Loss of financial security is frequently a cause of concern, whether it is a real danger or not. During a sharp drop in the stock market, for example, when interest rates were soaring, a young businessman was terrified of having certain loans called that would result in the loss of the working capital necessary to support his new business, and perhaps even make it impossible for him to meet the mortgage payments on his home. It was a legitimate concern. Feeling overwhelmed, he became agitated and depressed. He could not sleep and was irritable and abrupt. His continual preoccupation with the possibility of loss had made it impossible for him to think of any solutions that would prevent the loss. The psychiatrist pointed out to him that his worrying about the problem was blocking his ability to deal with it. His dread was rooted in a fear of losing control, while his efforts to retain control were progressively more self-defeating. His frantic anger had already alienated several business colleagues who might have been of help to him. The therapist aggressively reviewed the actual facts of the matter with him, including the details of the patient's financial situation; he agreed with him that there was a serious risk, but helped him gain perspective by pointing up certain compensating factors the patient had lost sight of. He emphasized that the patient's desperation to regain control was serving him poorly. As the immediate issue became decentralized, the patient's fear and hopelessness subsided, allowing him not only to feel better but also to consider realistic options.

In the process of decentralizing the depressive focus, the therapist often has to take what is called a paradigmatic position—agreeing with the patient that his special concern is legitimate, so that they can become allies in its solution. Then the therapist proceeds beyond the problem at hand to an exploration of how the emotional state of the patient contributes to and aggravates his inability to cope.

A thirty-six-year-old woman consulted a psychiatrist when she learned that her husband was involved with another woman and intended to seek a divorce. "I can't live without him. Our marriage is all that has meant anything to me. I keep writing him notes, but he doesn't answer. I called him at his hotel yesterday and he just hung up on me. I want him back so desperately!" The paradigmatic response of her therapist begins: "I know how much this loss must mean to you. I can understand why you want him back. Life must seem meaningless to you right now." She concurs. But then he shifts ground: "It's remarkable how out of touch you are with your anger toward him. It must infuriate you that he has rejected you. My hunch is that you have been controlled by him for a much longer time than you realize." He now alerts her to her underlying anger, and, at the same time, she begins to see that the husband in whom she has invested so much love and dependency is a little less lovable.

The therapist is also moving to accomplish three other goals at the same time. First, he is creating an opportunity for her to release both the grief she feels and the anger that has accumulated within her. Secondly, he is offering her some relief from her guilt, since he knows that at some level she feels primarily responsible for what has happened. At this moment she is not likely to see the dissolution of her marriage as the result of a progressively demoralizing interaction between herself and her husband. Being depressed, she is more apt to assume that she has failed, has done something seriously wrong to warrant such rejection. Finally, the therapist is beginning to restore some of her self-esteem.

The release of emotions, of guilt, and the restoration of self-esteem are recurrent themes throughout both short- and long-term therapy of the depressed person.

When Marian Johnson was referred by her family doctor to a psychiatrist for therapy, she was completely unaware of the connection between her emotions and her physical distress. Shortly after the birth of her first child she had begun to suffer from headaches and dizzy spells. She was afraid that she might have a brain tumor. In spite of a completely negative medical checkup, she still had serious doubts about the state of her health. Reluctantly she began therapy, stating, "Of course I'm unhappy. I don't think there's any hope for me unless the doctors can find something physically wrong to explain the way I feel. I can't work; I can't take care of my house or my baby. I can't do anything the way I am."

In taking her history, the therapist soon learned that Marian had been through a series of traumatic events in a short space of time. Her father had been operated on for a benign tumor four weeks before she delivered her baby. Shortly after the child's birth, her husband became preoccupied with business problems and showed little or no sexual interest in her. Her mother frequently accused her of not taking adequate care of the baby. At times her mother was frankly brutal, making such remarks as, "You're a lousy mother. And you're pigheaded too." And again, "You just don't want to take any advice from anyone. You have always been selfish and ungrateful."

As Marian spoke, hesitantly and only with encouragement, about these experiences, her eyes filled up with tears. "I couldn't stand it if anything happened to my father," she admitted. Again, tearfully, she confessed to feeling rejected by her husband. "I don't know why he doesn't take any interest in me sexually. I know that there isn't anyone else; he's not the type. But at night he hardly speaks to me. He just reads and watches television and goes to bed."

Her mother proved to have been a chronic problem for her, frequently berating both her father and her, making her feel useless and unattractive. When she was in high school, her mother repeatedly compared her unfavorably with other girls. "Why can't you get any interesting boy friends?" And "Why did Sarah win the French competition instead of you?" To compensate for her feelings of inadequacy, Marian had worked compulsively to win the highest academic record she could. She became perfectionistic, but in spite of her efforts she never received any praise from her mother. Nor was she allowed to express unhappiness. If she tried, her mother took her comments as a personal accusation and retaliated cruelly.

As her emotions surfaced, her physical distress gradually decreased. Again and again the therapist would have to ask "What do you feel about this?" and "What do you feel about that?" since Marian was simply not used to being able to understand and express emotions. This was particularly true of anger. "Has anything happened since your last visit that might have made you angry?" the therapist would ask, gently, patiently, knowing that her initial denial would be followed later by a slow recollection of an incident or two that "might have angered me," and finally, "yes, that did anger me."

From time to time she became angry with the therapist but found it painfully difficult to admit it. Once, for instance, he was fifteen minutes late for her session. This annoyed her because she had made a dental appointment following her visit, and she would now either lose some of her therapy time or be late for the dentist. She felt too guilty to express her predicament frankly. "How can I get angry at you after all you've done for me?" she asked. The therapist pointed out: "Why not? No matter how close a relationship may be, or how good it is, it has to allow for the privilege of getting annoyed at times when the situation warrants it." This was a fundamentally different response from that to which she was accustomed from her family, and it served as a vital opportunity for her to learn a new way of experiencing and expressing feelings.

"You must learn to be more direct in stating your ideas and emotions," her therapist encouraged her. With his support she began to test herself with her husband. She gingerly confronted him one evening with her feelings of sexual rejection. At first he was surprised. He had not been aware of neglecting her, although he had. He admitted to just as much affection and desire for her as always, but attributed his fatigue and low spirits to pressures at work. For the first time he began to share with her what those pressures were. "I didn't want to tell you. I didn't want to upset you, with a new baby and all. As a matter of fact, since you were feeling so unwell, I thought you might have lost interest in sex."

Over a period of eight months, Marian's physical

symptoms disappeared. She realized that these had been caused by her depression. She also realized that, true to form, she had been reacting to her depression with guilt, as if she had been entirely responsible for it. When she was able to understand that her feelings of inferiority were in large measure caused by the undermining criticisms of her mother and were compounded by her inability to cope directly and immediately with feelings and events as they occurred, she began to feel more self-confident and worth while.

A certain amount of humor is a vital asset in psychotherapy. Psychiatrist Lawrence Kubie warned against the injudicious use of humor in therapy lest it be at the expense of the patient and reinforce his low self-esteem, but he also pointed out that it can "express true warmth and affection" as well. "The critical difference is between laughing *with* someone or laughing at them. . . . In the hands of an experienced therapist, humor can be a safe and effective tool." What Kubie was cautioning against is a particular kind of humor that puts down either the therapist or the patient, especially as it might be employed by a beginning therapist or a therapist who uses it as an outlet for his own hostilities. This is consistent with Freud's concept that hostility is the basis of wit. Nonetheless, humor is a vital and necessary response to certain situations and an important counterbalance to depression. Humor restores and enlarges perspective. One middle-aged businessman, speaking with great earnestness, said to his therapist: "These have been the most difficult months I've ever had in business. Profit margins cut. Employee problems. Patent suits. But, damn it, in spite of everything, I've maintained my insanity throughout!" When he and the therapist realized his slip, they both laughed, together.

It is difficult to convey with words an accurate picture of what happens over a period of time in psychotherapy. As a result, it has been easy for the public to misconstrue the nature of the therapeutic experience. Certain aspects of psychotherapy have been extracted and seized upon, in a somewhat simplistic way, as the cornerstone of treatment. Free the patient from his sexual guilt. Help the patient to be able to express his anger outwardly and immediately. Each of these goals is basically relevant in the therapy of the depressed individual, but the popular assumption that the "cured" person should be capable of hopping into bed with anyone, anywhere, as a result of his newly acquired freedom from inhibitions, or that he should be able to yell and scream at members of his family at will, could not be farther from the truth.

It is generally true that the depressed person does have difficulty in expressing his anger when provoked. Sometimes, because of tension, he is irritable and reacts with too quick a temper. In the course of therapy he will be encouraged to find new and better ways to handle hostility—ways that do not omit judicious self-control when it is indicated. If, as in the case of Marian Johnson, the patient has been seriously out of touch with his feelings, he will become more aware of what he is experiencing when he is experiencing it. If justifiably angered, he will begin to see how anger can serve a useful purpose.

Frank Jensen found it very difficult to become

angry at, or to set limits for, his fourteen-year-old son. He was patient and understanding to a fault. In contrast to many of his friends who had alienated their teen-age children by refusing to listen to them and by pressing their own ideas and demands on them unreasonably, he had always tried to maintain a tolerant and open relationship with his son that afforded the two of them some degree of closeness. However, when the boy began coming home later than allowed, skipping school several times, and using his allowance money to buy beer against his parents' wishes, the problem of defiance only became worse as his father spent hours trying to talk to his son and coax him into complying with family rules. One evening, in a peak of anger, the father shouted: "If you come in one more night after the time limit without calling, that will be the end of your allowance!" It was the last such incident. The boy had been asking for limits and for some show of feeling to indicate that his parents intended to enforce those limits. Because of the basically sound relationship with his father, he had been able to respond to this demand without becoming alienated.

Anger, at the right time and when honestly provoked, can serve a vital purpose. But therapy is not designed to help the formerly depressed individual become a bundle of rage. Much of the anger that the patient gradually becomes aware of and releases in therapy is either stored up from previous failures to deal with it or has been the result of a misinterpretation of events around him.

Many depressed individuals have always been very dependent on positive feedback from the environment in order to bolster, again and again, a secure sense of their own worth. School is an ideal setting for such feedback. If intelligent enough, the youngster can work hard to obtain good grades. If athletically inclined, he can put his energies into becoming a star basketball or football player. Once school days have passed, it becomes much more difficult to obtain evidence of one's value from the environment. How can you measure it? By the amount of money earned? By the number of times each day one's husband or wife says "I love you?" By the number of invitations to social events one receives?

As the opportunities for positive feedback diminish, the opportunities for rejection increase. The world is so complex and so busy that it can hardly attend to the normal sensitivities of people, much less to those of people who are in greater need of ego reassurance than others. The self-concern of the depressed person sets him up to interpret as rejection what is only indifference, and as indifference what is sometimes actually a considerable amount of respect and affection. He is easily hurt. He can easily become angry as a result of feeling slighted.

Anger that is rooted in his sensitivity will be released in the therapeutic session, although he will certainly not be encouraged to release it wildly elsewhere. Rather, the emphasis will be on helping him to more correctly determine his own worth and set free his self-esteem from its compelling dependency on what others think or say about him. In this way, there will be fewer hurts and hence fewer opportunities for anger.

The depressed person's tendency to procrastinate,

not only in activities and decision-making but also in responding to any stimuli, serves as a further source of frustration and anger. "I meant to place the order sooner," said a patient who worked as purchasing agent for a large company, "but I was slow in getting around to it. By the time I made the call, I was told there would be a five-week delay in delivery. Damn it, I was furious. I told them that if they valued our business they'd better have it there in two weeks. It ended up taking eight weeks, and cost us several thousand in lost orders. At first it was a matter of pride. Now, after our talks, I see that it was really a matter of my dragging my feet on the order for over a month. Why did I do that? I had plenty of time. Do you think it had anything to do with the idea I have of not being properly appreciated by top management for the job I do?"

Therapy is a series of reconsiderations, a reappraisal of feelings and experiences in a different light. As the emotional turmoil surrounding the acute phase of depression lessens, the patient and the therapist have a chance to explore the core premises on which the patient's perception of experience rests. An Adlerian technique for discovering such premises rapidly and releasing some of the emotions attached to them is to ask the patient what his earliest memory of life is, the earliest memory he can recall at that particular moment.

"I was sleeping on a mattress in my parents' bedroom. They had moved me out of my crib, and the junior bed hadn't arrived yet. I was torn between wanting to have the crib back, wanting to stay on the mattress in their room, and wanting to grow up and move into a bigger bed of my own." This patient repeatedly reacted to major changes in his life with a paralyzing ambivalence, never sure of which direction to take and painfully weighing the alternatives again and again.

"I was in nursery school. The teacher asked how many of the children still slept in cribs. I put up my hand. Only one other little girl did the same. I was humiliated. It hurt. I was angry at myself and my parents for keeping me a child." In her adult years this woman remained extremely sensitive to humiliation, often experiencing it when it wasn't warranted, and reacting to it with outbursts of rage.

"I was on a tricycle, pedaling quickly down the street away from the house. I was running away. Something had happened between my mother and me. I was being punished for something, I don't recall what. I was angry, hurt." In adult life, this patient reacted to any show of hostility toward him, however mild, by withdrawing. Sometimes he would become silent for hours. Sometimes he would stay out late at night or disappear for a few days after a disagreement with his wife.

"I recall Mommy coming home. I must have been three. I remember she had just arrived from the hospital. She had been away for so long, and she had been so sick. I ran and hugged her. It was so good to have her back again." This patient revealed a high degree of sensitivity to loss, but an ability to give freely and warmly of love and concern.

There are a number of such themes that run

throughout an individual's psychological make-up, and in the course of therapy there are numerous opportunities to explore them. "I just don't like to talk to my brother," said one man. "I don't approve of his behavior. His sister-in-law had a drinking problem. She still does. He won't let her in the house and doesn't like the idea of his wife's having too much contact with her own sister. I consider his behavior selfish. I think he ought to help. It's downright immoral." The therapist suggested another way to observe and interpret the brother's attitude: Had he considered the possibility that his brother had his own equilibrium to maintain? The patient had already mentioned that his brother had had several episodes of depression over the years, one of which required hospitalization. "I often have to advise people to set limits on how much they can be expected to do for others without compromising their own health or well-being," the psychiatrist informed him. After some thought the patient concurred that he had been unreasonably harsh in looking at his brother's behavior. This reconsideration also opened the way for an analysis of his own value system and the extent to which his own depression and feelings of guilt were rooted in a rigid and punitive evaluation of his own behavior.

Throughout the entire course of therapy the psychiatrist must carefully assess and balance how he will fill the dependency needs of the patient without inviting an excessive dependency that would prolong and complicate the recovery process. Anyone who is afraid and feeling helpless is bound to become more dependent than usual. He is likely to invest this need in the doctor, the person to whom he turns for relief. The structure of therapy—regular visits with an understanding person who is helpful—as well as the opportunity to focus on troubling issues are both going to produce a certain amount of self-generative dependency.

There is a relationship between the number of visits per week to the therapist and the amount of dependency that builds up. A patient who has only one or two sessions a week is not likely to become as dependent as one who sees the therapist every day. Carefully defining the amount of time the therapist and patient will spend together—an hour, a half hour —provides a sense of security and sets a limit on the amount of dependency that may develop.

Dependency needs are aggravated when any relationship, including therapy, is riddled with inconsistencies and ambivalence. One patient, a young woman, kept changing appointments and canceling them at the last moment in an unconscious attempt to prevent herself from becoming too involved in therapy. Paradoxically, she was creating a state of uncertainty that reinforced her fears and consequently made her feel more helpless.

In the beginning, the average depressed person sees the therapist once or twice a week, as a rule, for sessions running about forty-five minutes. Once a sufficient degree of well-being has been established, the subsequent frequency of visits will be determined by how much there is to talk about, how much turmoil there still is in the patient's life, and how much room there is for further insight. Throughout therapy, because of his susceptibility to developing strong needs for those with whom he is involved, the depressed individual will often struggle with the desire to see the doctor more often and, on the other hand, with the impulse to terminate therapy at the earliest possible moment.

One of the therapist's most difficult tasks is encouraging the patient to break out of patterns of behavior that are self-defeating and damaging. This may require a considerable amount of persuasion and patience on the part of the therapist. A few patients stop the behavior as soon as they realize that it is injurious. Many, however, tend to procrastinate because they do not see the point of the advice given, or because they are unwilling to forfeit the satisfaction they mistakenly believe their behavior affords them. It is usually not enough for the therapist to recommend a change. He must also point out to the patient that such a change will provoke some depression, but will at the same time release emotions that can be worked through in their sessions. The patient who has been compulsively engaged in a series of empty sexual relationships, for example, may be concealing a great deal of insecurity about himself as a person.

Many depressed patients can be successfully treated without involving their families in any significant way. It is always a help, if patient and family agree, for the therapist to meet key members of the family to determine for himself something about the nature of their relationships with the patient. The family, after all, is a group of powerfully interrelated people who have contributed to, and are affected by, the patient's depression. No one is depressed in a self-contained vacuum. And, as the British psychiatrist Ronald D. Laing has pointed out in *The Politics of the Family*, the patient is often the representative of the pathology that runs through the entire family. His recovery must necessarily cause waves—shifts in the values and the balance of power of the entire group.

One of the two most common situations in which the therapist will involve himself more actively with the family is in the treatment of a depressed person whose marital difficulties have contributed to, or have been caused by, the depression. The second is the treatment of an adolescent, in which some initial contact with the family is necessary to evaluate the environment and obtain a thorough history of the problem.

The therapist of the depressed adolescent rarely counsels the teen-ager's family, since such contact could jeopardize the trust and confidence the adolescent may have placed, slowly and painfully, in this unusual adult who listens. There is too much risk of losing that trust through too much contact with the parents. When necessary, the family members are often referred to a social worker or a colleague of the therapist for counseling.

It is common, however, for the therapist to work with the husband or wife of the depressed individual, not only to help the partner understand how better to relate to the patient, but also to modify attitudes and behavior patterns that may have contributed to the depression in the first place. Occasionally, to improve the communication between patient and spouse, both are seen together in a number of joint sessions after the patient's depression has lifted.

From time to time the relative makes himself completely unavailable to the therapist. Such resistance is common when a marriage has deteriorated to the point where divorce is imminent. Sometimes the other partner feels that there is something he cannot or will not reveal. He may feel humiliated or guilty, often without cause, by the thought of being somehow responsible for the patient's depression. He may be afraid that the doctor will find "something wrong" with him, too. He may be unwilling to relinquish his position in the "I'm O.K., you're not O.K." balance in the marriage. Frequently, he does not know what therapy is all about and hence why he should be involved in it at all.

Once the patient has recovered from the depression, the final decision is when to terminate regular visits. "Am I ready to stop seeing you?" the patient may ask, or the therapist may suggest, "I think it's time to cut back on our visits." Often the patient's decision is affected by external considerations, such as leaving town, taking a vacation, becoming too busy at work to continue regular sessions. When this happens, it is important that the decision crystallize rather than drift into being through default.

The end of therapy is not the end of the relationship between therapist and patient. Each remains open to the other, and should the occasion arise in the future for the patient to come again—with a problem, an idea, an experience to tell about—the therapist remains available to renew communication. Freud, in his paper "Analysis Terminable and Interminable," wrote in a different age of a different process. In the course of analysis, a point should be reached, he emphasized, at which the analysis ends. Using the criterion of change in the patient's personality or the emergence of resistances that could not be worked through, the analyst, he felt, should call it quits. Enough is enough.

Unfortunately, the Freudian concept of ending therapy was a more or less final one. Unless the patient were to consider re-entering analysis, the door to his analyst's consulting room was effectively closed. The result of this policy was that many a patient who had to struggle through life crises *subsequent* to a long period of analysis was denied the brief counseling that would have helped him meet the particular difficulties with greater resilience. Preventive psychiatry—which includes keeping the recovered patient in good shape —had not yet been born.

Currently, it is an increasingly common practice for the therapist to encourage the patient to keep in contact with him. In this way he can keep track of what has been going on in the patient's life, so that in the event of a future crisis he will have the knowledge necessary to be of further help.

How long does therapy take?

A week. A month. Six months. Three years.

There are many factors that determine the duration of therapy and its outcome: How long had the patient been depressed before starting therapy? To what extent has he complicated his life by building traps? How stable and supportive is his present life situation? How flexible is he? How quickly does he learn? How skilled and experienced is the therapist in dealing with depression? The answers to questions such as these will influence the amount of therapy required for any particular person. For example, if he has serious marital difficulties or has positioned himself in a job that is essentially demoralizing, therapy may go on much longer than if his depression is a simple and uncomplicated reaction to a stressful situation, such as the death of an elderly parent.

Psychotherapy offers the depressed person the opportunity to free himself from his depression and, at the same time, gain valuable and useful insights. In recent years, this process has been accelerated by means of tricyclic antidepressant drugs.

7

A
Breakthrough
with
Antidepressant
Drugs

A MAJOR BREAKTHROUGH in the treatment of depression took place in 1957, when tricyclic antidepressant drugs —called tricyclic because of their three-ring chemical structure—were discovered. Until then, there were no drugs available that would conveniently and effectively relieve depression. Tranquilizers such as the phenothiazines had been introduced a few years earlier and, although they had proved useful in the treatment of severe emotional disorders, such as schizophrenia, and of milder tension states, they had no influence on mood.

As with many other medical breakthroughs, the tricyclic antidepressants were discovered by accident. The Swiss psychiatrist Ronald Kuhn was attempting to see whether this group of compounds, which chemically somewhat resemble the phenothiazines, might also be useful in relieving the acute emotional symptoms of schizophrenia. They were not. But in the process of his study, he noted a significant alleviation of depression in many patients. Because of the fact that it required about three weeks of regular use for these drugs to relieve depression, his observations were initially met with considerable skepticism. His findings were attributed to what is called "the placebo effect."

The placebo effect is essentially a change in a person's physical or emotional state induced by the use of a biologically inert substance that the recipient assumes will help him to feel better. "I will give you an injection of this new medication," the doctor suggests, "and within a few minutes your headache will go away." Frequently it does, even though the injection consists of little more than water and salt. The placebo effect must always be considered whenever claims are made that a substance produces a psychological change. People are suggestible—some more than others—and will respond to the combination of what is done to them and what the physician says is being done in a more or less compliant way, depending on the amount of trust they place in the doctor and the extent to which they are receptive to suggestion.

Evaluation of the tricyclic antidepressants required carefully executed "double-blind" studies (in which the evaluators of the tests are unaware of which substance is being given to each patient, and in which the patients to be tested have been selected on a random basis) to establish once and for all that somehow the drugs effectively relieved depression—not in all the patients, but in the majority.

Prior to the discovery of these antidepressants, there were really only four alternatives open to the depressed individual. If severely depressed, he might receive electric shock treatments. If mildly depressed, he might receive central-nervous-system stimulants, such as amphetamines; more often, unless he underwent a lengthy psychoanalysis, he received no help at all. Many patients whose psychoanalyses extended over a period of years were actually struggling with depression. Had antidepressant drugs been available, the course of their therapy could have been dramatically shortened.

For years, amphetamines were given liberally to patients for the relief of low spirits and fatigue. Not infrequently, they were combined with barbiturates to quell nervousness and anxiety. Not only was this approach unjustified and ineffective in relieving depression, but the widespread misuse of these drugs contributed substantially toward the current epidemic of drug dependency. Taking pep pills to get started in the morning or to stay awake at night to study or work, and then gulping down sleeping tablets of one kind or another to quiet tension, relax, and sleep for ten or twelve hours became a way of life for millions of Americans.

The barbiturates—like alcohol—are central-nervous-system depressants and often intensify depression, especially when used over a period of time. Amphetamines do not relieve depression; what they actually do is cause a transient increase in energy usually associated with a decrease in mental efficiency and judgment. As their effects wear off, they are often followed by episodes of severe depression, as the central nervous system attempts to rebound from the abnormal provocation and regain some kind of equilibrium.

It is no coincidence that amphetamines and barbiturates are among the most widely abused drugs today, while the antidepressants are rarely, if ever, abused. The former drugs produce an immediate response; the antidepressants do not produce euphoria, and their effectiveness against depression takes place slowly, over a period of weeks. Furthermore, if a person is not depressed, the antidepressants usually have no effect at all on mood or emotions.

The special character of the antidepressants is that in order to work an adequate dose must be given over a sufficient period of time. The average daily dose of a drug such as imipramine (Tofranil) or amitriptyline (Elavil) is 150 milligrams. Some patients require only half that dose; others require somewhat more. Even in the correct dosage, the drug takes about three or four weeks to work. Why this is so is still unknown. A parallel situation is seen in the use of hormones to correct endocrine disturbances. In the treatment of hypothyroidism, a number of months of thyroid hormone administration is required to restore to normal the indices of thyroid function—the basal metabolic rate or protein-bound iodine level. It requires many weeks of estrogen therapy to restore the hormonal balance to normal when the problem has been related to estrogen deficiency. The antidepressants must somehow activate a cycle of biochemical activity, such as a shift in the distribution of minerals and the metabolism of biogenic amines in the brain, which requires a certain period of time to take place.

The typical depressed individual who is given an antidepressant shows some lifting of mood and increased energy during the very first week of therapy. Within a few nights he is sleeping better. He may or may not notice the changes himself, or the improvement may be noticeable only to observers. During the second week of treatment there is often a plateau; no further changes are noted, and sometimes there is a recurrence of emotional distress. By the end of the third week of treatment the patient usually begins to feel better. His concentration is more effective. He has fewer episodes of depression, and they are often short-lived. When a disturbing event or provocative remark upsets him, he seems to rebound from the distress much more quickly than before.

How long should the individual continue to take antidepressant medication? Some patients, especially those who have never been depressed before and whose reactions are of relatively short duration—a few months, say—may soon be able to reduce their daily dose of imipramine or amitriptyline and may terminate the medication within four or five months. Others who have been chronically depressed for years, or who have a history of recurrent episodes of depression, may have to continue taking small doses of the antidepressant drugs for a year or two. A handful of patients may continue to use the drugs for years, either on a regular basis or for periods of a few months from time to time when depressive episodes recur in the setting of new stresses.

There is a very good chance that the nature of antidepressant drugs is not "antidepressant" at all.

Their effect may be more on the intensity and tenacity of the mood change than on its quality. In other words, if a person is depressed, it may well be that biologically the treatments do nothing to influence the mood itself, but rather affect the electrical and biochemical aspects of brain function, reactivating the resilience mechanisms so that he is able to rebound from his depression and regain his normal mood.

This hypothesis is strengthened by the observation that many people who are taking antidepressant drugs still experience appropriate reactions of sadness or distress to upsetting events. "The real difference in my reactions since I've been on this medication is that I don't stay down as long as I did. At first, of course, I slept better and ate better. Bit by bit, I started feeling less paralyzed. Now, if I get upset, I get over it faster. Last night, for instance, my mother called. She made me feel guilty for not calling her. I started knotting up inside. But when the conversation was over, it was over. I didn't dwell on it as I used to."

As with all drugs, antidepressants have side effects, although these are rarely serious. The most common side effects are excessive perspiration and constipation, the latter resulting from a drying up of the mucous membranes of the intestinal tract. Many patients complain of a dry mouth, particularly when they are tense. Some notice lightheadedness, because of a transient drop in blood pressure, when they stand up quickly. Others experience fatigue, sleepiness, skin rashes, sensitivity to sunlight. Most of the uncomfortable side effects occur within the first ten days of treatment and subside thereafter. They are also dose-related, usually disappearing in a day or so with a reduction in the dosage of the drug.

Many patients gain weight while taking antidepressants. Carefully controlled studies substantiate that this weight gain is caused by an increased food intake, probably the result of a better appetite. At one time it was argued that the weight loss accompanying depression reflected a breakdown and excretion of body tissue that took place regardless of food intake. Recently, diet books have cautioned readers against using antidepressants while trying to lose weight, implying that the drugs themselves directly effect a gain in weight. The studies have proved both assumptions incorrect.

The experience and judgment of the physician are critical in his decision as to whether to give an antidepressant. If he feels that the patient will pull out of his depression rapidly, he may refrain from giving a course of drug therapy that takes about four weeks to work and normally runs several months. He also wants to be sure that the patient who says he is depressed really *is*. Some patients who describe themselves as being depressed are not; others who deny it are.

There is considerable variation in the resilience with which different people rebound from depression once they have made a decision to get professional help and have had a few therapy sessions. A thirty-year-old woman was seen in consultation because she complained of being depressed. She had recently broken up with her fiancé; prior to that she had never been significantly depressed. During the first two sessions, her therapist was able to elicit the hurt and anger she had felt in response to the end of her affair. "Even though I ended it, I felt rejected," she pointed out. By the third visit she was in much better spirits and was sleeping well. The rapid disappearance of her depression made the psychiatrist defer prescribing anti-depressants, keeping them in reserve in case the depressive mood returned. By contrast, another woman who presented the same psychiatrist with a five-year history of insomnia, pessimism, irritability, social withdrawal, and a poor sex life, and who had never considered herself depressed until she read about depression in a popular magazine, was put on antidepressant medication after her second visit. The psychiatrist's decision in this case was governed by the long-standing nature of her depression and the fact that psychotherapy alone was unlikely to modify such a chronic pattern.

Treatment with antidepressants will also be influenced by the complexity of the patient's depression. If the patient has a relatively uncomplicated depression—a lowering of mood, some anxiety, insomnia, and weight loss—the physician can expect a good response to the drugs. However, the patient may also demonstrate a great deal of fear, agitation, and restlessness; or the lowered mood may be associated with hypersensitivity approaching the paranoid: "Sometimes I think that everyone is out to get me. In fact, even this morning the phone rang three times and there was no one on the other end." Intense anger— even at times to the point of physical violence—may be part of the picture. In these circumstances, the psychiatrist may add to the regime of antidepressant medication a major tranquilizer, usually of the phenothiazine group, which by itself does not relieve depression but which will bring rage, fear, sexual unrest, hypersensitivity, and agitation under control within a few days. In fact, at times, if he does not prescribe a combination of the two drugs he will discover that the patient will not recover as anticipated by the end of four weeks of treatment because of the impact of these emotions.

The attitudes of both doctor and patient are important to the success of psychopharmacological treatment. Many therapists have not been able to integrate the psychological and pharmacological approaches to depression. Some insist on the psychogenic origin of depression; others, on its biological causes. The former group tends to withhold medication, even when it is clearly indicated; if and when they finally recommend it, their interest in continuing psychotherapeutic treatment seems to atrophy. "When I was first seeing the doctor, he wanted two sessions a week. After three months he started me on a drug. A week later he cut me to half an hour once a week, without any explanation." The organicists tend to interview the patient briefly and offer medication, but have little interest in exploring with him the psychological or environmental factors in his depression. The fact that a large number of patients are seen by professionals who do not have the right to prescribe—psychologists, social workers, the clergy—poses a special problem. They are reluctant to recommend medication for fear that the physician giving it will intrude on their treatment relationship. Unless a collaborative, competition-free environment exists between these professionals and the physician, many depressed patients in need of antidepressant medication will not receive it unless a major crisis develops.

Does a doctor's conviction that a drug works—or his skepticism—affect the outcome of antidepressant treatment? It has been clearly established that suggestion plays an important role in the effectiveness of drugs that are designed to reduce anxiety and tension. Hence the popularity of the minor tranquilizers and over-the-counter preparations used for calming nerves. A senior psychiatrist at a leading English hospital had a reputation for obtaining remarkable results from a variety of drugs. When he would inquire, in a most authoritative tone, "You are getting better, aren't you?" a patient would usually find himself replying, "Yes, sir, if you say so, sir!"

The time lag in the effects produced by the antidepressants, the tenacious nature of chronic depression, and the double-blind studies of these drugs argue strongly against any significant influence of the placebo effect in their use. The doctor's attitude, however, can and will influence how the patient uses the medication. If he is skeptical and considers the drug relatively unimportant, the patient may pick up this message and respond to it by skipping doses of the drug, stopping it before it has had time to work, or denying flatly that his improved outlook has anything to do with the medication. This, of course, will enhance the ego of many psychotherapists, who can then feel that their psychotherapeutic efforts have been the exclusive cause for improvement.

The convinced physician can err by promising too much, thereby activating the curious negativism of many depressed individuals. Even though they are reaching out for help, something within them wants to preserve their depressed state—the control it has afforded them over others, the sympathy it has elicited, the anger it expresses for which they know no other outlet. If the therapist is too enthusiastic in offering relief through medication, he may stir up this unconscious resistance to recovery. "After I took the first pill at bedtime, I could feel the effect," said one patient who had been promised a rapid improvement through medication. "I couldn't sleep. The next day I was washed out, but I continued to use it as the doctor said I should. My legs felt weak, and I thought I was going to collapse.

"I called the doctor three times the next night. He told me to stop the drug and come by the next day for another prescription. I did. This was supposed to be a milder form of antidepressant. But I felt even worse. The day after I started on it I couldn't get out of bed at all. My legs were shaky—so weak I had to hold onto the furniture to get to the bathroom. I called him again, and this time he told me to come in for a special appointment to discuss the problem.

"When I saw him he told me that most of the changes I complained about could not possibly be part of the drug effect, and in the course of the discussion I realized that I was really reluctant to give up the subtle way in which I had been able to get out hostility toward my wife—without giving her fair grounds for retaliation—by being tired and depressed around the house in the evenings and on week ends. If the drug really worked, I was going to lose that outlet and have to learn a new way of coping with the anger she stirred up in me."

Many patients are reluctant to take a drug to improve their mood because they are afraid of the implications of dependency. Some are afraid of becoming dependent on the drug. Others feel that if they take a drug the change in their mood will be artificial, that any improvement that occurs will not be "real." One patient, for instance, was unconsciously so afraid of becoming dependent on anyone or anything that he would cancel every other appointment with his therapist at the last minute, having suddenly discovered that he had another commitment. It took nearly three months, during which time the patient became progressively less afraid of being dependent, before the therapist could even suggest the use of antidepressants. Even then the patient was infuriated, interpreting the recommendation as a personal rejection. Another patient reported that since he had been taking antidepressants, his wife had become afraid that his emotions might somehow be synthetic. "Would you still love me," she asked, "if you weren't on Tofranil?"

Knowing when to start an antidepressant drug is much easier than knowing when to stop. Obviously, if after four weeks there is no improvement, the doctor may have misjudged either the indications for the drug or the resistance factors in the patient. If it has worked, the two important guidelines are the frequency and recurrence of depressions in the past, as well as their severity, and the extent to which the patient has worked through his own inner conflicts and adjusted the environmental factors contributing to his depression. If, for example, the patient had been quite disturbed and perhaps suicidal when treatment began, the physician would be likely to continue the drug treatment for many months until he felt that there had been a sufficient change in the patient's attitudes to warrant stopping. If a patient has had a marital problem or difficulties in his work situation and these have settled down, and he has begun to reflect on his own contributions to his trap-building, then the physician may begin trying to reduce the medication and eventually terminate it.

In some instances of more serious depression, where there is a long history of tenacious or recurrent depression, the patient may be encouraged to stay on maintenance doses of the antidepressant drug for years. Recently, psychiatrist Ronald Fieve and others have advocated the continued use of a lithium salt, a drug originally introduced over twenty years ago by the Australian psychiatrist J. F. Cade for the treatment of manic excitements, to prevent recurrences of depression. The effectiveness of lithium in alleviating the emotional changes and behavioral aspects of manic states—the grandiosity of thinking, the overactivity, the egomania, the anger and irritability—has been well established, along with its usefulness in preventing recurrences of mania. In a small number of patients diagnosed as manic-depressive, it is possible that the long-term administration of lithium may also prevent recurrent episodes of depression. However, there is no reason to assume that lithium has any beneficial effect in the treatment or prevention of depression when it is unipolar; that is, when it lacks a manic component.

Other drugs for the management of depression besides the tricyclic antidepressants have been proposed from time to time. The drugs called monoamine oxidase inhibitors were shown at one time to be useful in a small and special group of depressed patients. These compounds were abandoned partly because of their limited usefulness compared to the tricyclics, and also because of the high frequency of dangerous side effects, particularly on the liver and the cardiovascular system.

On an experimental basis only, endocrine substances such as the thyroid hormone, the thyroid-stimulating hormone, and triiodothyronine, a derivative of the thyroid hormone, have been said to possess antidepressant properties. Currently, thyroid hormones are added to tricyclic antidepressants by some physicians to facilitate the effect of these drugs. Estrogens have been tested, without success, on depressed women around the time of menopause. Many women using birth-control pills, which are in essence hormones affecting the menstrual cycle and ovulation, have reported a lowering of mood when taking the pill. That a link exists between variations in mood and alterations in endocrine functions seems apparent, but what this link is and how it can be exploited in the interests of therapy remain to be clarified.

Tricyclic antidepressants have quietly revolutionized the treatment of depression. They have also underscored the importance of the role of biological factors in depression. And they have made it easier for the depressed person to resolve the psychological and environmental conflicts that are central to his mood.

8
Sex
as
a
Barometer

SEXUALITY AND SELF-ESTEEM are closely connected. In this culture, with its *Playboy* and *Penthouse* magazines and sex therapy clinics, physical attractiveness and the ability to perform in bed have become serious ego issues.

In the first half of the twentieth century, the focus of male-female relationships in the United States was marriage, and the emphasis in marriage was placed on the social and economic integrity of the family group. The raising of children was of primary concern. Interpersonal compatibility was vaguely relevant, and both husband and wife had their respective roles to play no matter how they regarded the quality of the marriage itself.

In the last twenty years there has been a strong

127

shift in emphasis toward the importance of the intimate, personal nature of the relationship between a
man and a woman: their ability to communicate, to
form a trusting and sharing commitment, to sustain
romantic and sexual interest over a period of years.
"I wouldn't marry someone if he didn't turn me on"
has replaced the previous generation's expectation, "I
wouldn't marry someone if he wasn't dependable."

The growing demand for intimacy and sexual fulfillment in human relationships, both heterosexual and
homosexual, arises in part from the rejection of a culture in which the roles people played took precedence
over the importance of being themselves. It also reflects
the demise of family life, with parents, grandparents,
and adolescents all inhabiting their own separate
worlds. In spite of crowdedness, loneliness is epidemic.
The average individual feels isolated and alienated,
and these feelings reinforce the need for, and challenge
of, intimacy. A young man and woman standing naked
in the bedroom must encounter each other in immediate and uncamouflaged terms—sexually and emotionally—without roles, without social props, without ori-
entation to past and future.

This moment is made even more difficult because
of the profound depersonalization fostered by this
culture. "We try to make our employees feel like people, not numbers," said a spokesman for International
Business Machines in a *New York Times* article. If
the company has succeeded, this unpatentable secret
should be shared at once with the millions of people
the computer has helped to feel like things. The transactional analysts use the term "thinging" to describe

the process of regarding people as if they were objects. The social scientists aptly describe this as a marketing society, and whether one is sitting in on a planning meeting at a large advertising firm or a conference of scientists, it is more than a little disquieting to hear people discussed statistically as if they were items for sale or rent.

The individual begins to feel like an object, "A living object, but no longer a person," wrote T. S. Eliot in *The Cocktail Party:*

> When you're dressed for a party
> And are going downstairs, with everything about you
> Arranged to support you in the role you have chosen,
> Then sometimes, when you come to the bottom step
> There is one step more than your feet expected
> And you come down with a jolt. Just for a moment
> You have the experience of being an object
> At the mercy of a malevolent staircase. . . .

In the general process of depersonalization, sex too has succumbed to "thinging." Because of the intimate connection between sex and self-esteem, the phenomenon of impersonal sex has catalyzed the spread of depression. Loneliness and a feeling of being alienated have become common ways of experiencing depression. At the same time, many lonely and depressed people turn to sex as a way of relieving that inner emptiness. Although the current culture places enormous value on sexual fulfillment, the underlying purpose of sexual encounters is often not sexual at all. During a period of low self-esteem, sexual conquests or the discovery of oneself as sexually desirable may temporarily ameliorate the feeling of being depressed;

yet there is usually a sharp return of depression afterward, when the bogus reassurance wears off. Under
such circumstances there can be no genuine ego
reinforcement.

Erik Erikson, in *Childhood and Society*, has
stressed the importance of experiencing sexual excitement and fulfillment within the framework of a relationship that also includes love, mutual trust, and a
sharing of the everyday concerns and activities of
living. The existentialist Martin Buber has outlined the
relevance of the I-Thou relationship as the basis for
real intimacy. Emotional closeness and a fulfilling sexual experience require the freedom to enter into a
"we" relationship, in which the I and the Thou become
one. The height of this experience, emotionally and
physically, is represented by the moment of orgasm,
which permits the individual to give up, for a few
moments, the ordinary boundaries of self and "dis-
solve" into a common bond with the loved partner.
Not every sexual experience has to have this unique
quality, but it will appear from time to time in the
sexual encounters of two people who love and care about
each other.

In order to allow oneself to participate in such a
union, two ingredients are essential: first, the individual
personality must be sufficiently intact to let go of itself
and promptly return after the experience is over. If
such a transitory giving up of ego boundaries is too
threatening to the person, the consequent fear will
block his ability to fully participate in the sexual experience. The second important element is trust, a
belief that the person with whom the sexual moment

is shared is also able and willing to give up the "I" for the sake of the "we." Trust is not created overnight. This kind of sexual experience is the product of hours and months of sharing many things other than sex, of setting the stage for a relationship in which intimacy and sex can be integrated.

Not all sexual encounters demand such a blending of personalities, but when a "quick roll in the hay" becomes the primary outlet for one's sexual drives, the inevitable enhancement of self-esteem that results from the complete experience does not occur and a slow, progressive waning in self-worth takes place, however it may be denied. "What is needed for sexual harmony," writes Simone de Beauvoir, "is not refinement in technique, but, rather, on the foundation of the moment's erotic charm, a mutual generosity of body and soul."

Nowhere is this concept of integrating the personal elements of the relationship with the sexual so important as in a relationship that is expected to endure over a period of time. Erotic attraction and sexual interest, if not backed up by love, fade rapidly. It is the caring, the interdependency, the openness in communication that exist between lovers that keep the erotic component vital and alive over a period of years.

Low self-esteem makes it difficult to find the kind of relatedness Erikson and Buber are talking about. In fact, when sexual encounters are used to combat unrecognized depression, one's sense of self-esteem is compromised even further.

Jane Conway, age twenty-nine, is a striking example of a young woman who became more and more depressed as she sought to find in sexual relationships what could be found only in a serious reconsideration of her worth as a person. She had always felt unattractive, which she was not, and unpopular with boys in school, which she was, since she clearly communicated her fear of, and disdain for, them.

Jane left home at nineteen and went to Boston, where she finished college and subsequently obtained a job as a computer programmer. She was usually cheerful and outgoing—as long as she was able to maintain a relationship with a man. Whenever she was without a regular boy friend, she was morose, lonely, unhappy, restless. She haunted singles' bars, where she would pick someone up and go to bed with him. Neither her regular sexual experiences nor these transient involvements led to orgasm. As long as she could prove to herself—over and over again—that she was attractive to men, she did not have to face the painful fear that she could never establish a more enduring love relationship with a man, since she felt basically unworthy of it.

Then for several years she had an affair with an older man for whom she worked. She knew she did not love him, but felt secure in his constant affection for her. However, she gradually grew bored with the relationship and, at times, was actually contemptuous of him. When he insisted on marriage, she ended the affair.

A year later she became involved with an emotionally erratic man who was grossly ambivalent in his attitude toward women. The more he confused her—"I love you, but you're not the kind of girl I want to spend my life with"—the more she felt she needed him. Again, her sexual experiences did not lead to orgasm.

At no time did Jane consider herself as chronically depressed. She saw her moods entirely as reactions to her life circumstances. It did not occur to her that she might benefit from professional guidance until she visited her physician because of recurrent intestinal difficulties and he suggested that she consult a psychiatrist.

In the course of several months of therapy, she rapidly assimilated the following insights: She had been battling against chronic depression and low self-esteem for years. She had a highly confused view of herself and her worth. Her father had always been a very withdrawn and unaffectionate man who gave little of himself to his family. As she grew up she desperately sought to find in her relationships with men what she had not found in her relationship with her father. As she progressed from one affair to another in search of the "perfect man," feeling empty and afraid when there was no man in her life, she used sex and her relationships with men as a temporary relief from her low self-esteem.

Jane had become an addict, in a sense, and the ultimate resolution of her difficulty included the termination of her sexual promiscuity as a way of restoring self-esteem, and the rediscovery of herself as a more complete person, with her own individuality, gaining the "I" in the Buber "I-Thou" equation.

A loss of sexual desire is one of the most common signs of depression. When this connection between sex and mood is missed, most people fear that something fundamental has happened to their sexual capacities. Many men and women in their forties and fifties, for example, mistakenly assume that the loss of sexual interest is the result of some kind of biological change associated with getting older. The sexual indifference of the depressed person can also be misinterpreted by his sexual partner as a loss of love and erotic attraction. Sometimes it is; more often it is not. There are many reasons why the depressed person loses an interest in sexual activity. Making him feel agitated, pessimistic, anxious, discouraged, the mood itself forces his attention away from sexual desire. His hypersensitivity to feeling rejected, his vulnerability to guilt, the difficulty he may have in releasing angry feelings, and sexual conflicts themselves combine to interfere with sexual drives.

Not all depressed people, however, lose their sexual desire. In fact, there are instances in which depression is associated with a heightening of sexual energy, a state referred to as sexual unrest. Sexual unrest is experienced as a direct stirring up of sexual urges. It is quite different from Jane Conway's essentially asexual attempt to gain self-esteem and ward off depression through sexual encounters. Sexual unrest may be due to hormonal changes but may also be the result of the anxiety and apprehension provoked in response to being depressed, since anxiety not uncommonly leads to a heightening in sexual urges.

A young woman who was somewhat depressed noticed a stirring up of sexual tension, caused by her fear and anxiety, whenever she felt overly pressured in preparing for college exams. Similarly, a fifty-three-

year-old man noted a sudden increase in the frequency
of his erections and the occurrence of a series of sexually exciting dreams, many of which led to spontaneous ejaculations. Some of these dreams were homosexual in content even though he had never had any
conscious homosexual impulses. He was deeply disturbed
by all this until, with the help of his physician, he was
able to relate it to a lowering of his mood that had
evolved over a number of months. He was concerned
about losing his energy and attractiveness. He was also
shaken by his daughter's liberal attitudes about sex and
the angry arguments they had had about their different
value systems. As his depression lifted, the unusual upsurge in his sexual drives subsided.

Many women who have experienced depression
after divorce and even after becoming widowed have
noted a stirring up of sexual drives that seems, to them,
somewhat out of keeping with their normal selves.
Unless these sexual feelings are related to a hypomanic
swing in mood—some people become mildly elated in
the process of denying depression—they are often experienced as uncomfortable and distracting rather than
pleasurable.

On the whole, however, depression is associated
with a loss of sexual interest. In certain instances this
loss reflects an unconscious hostility that is being expressed through the depression. Since people who are
depression-prone or in states of chronic depression
tend to withdraw into themselves when angry rather
than cope with the disturbing situation directly, the
withdrawal of sexual interest can be a highly effective
channel for the expression of hostility. "What Bill

doesn't realize," said his wife, "is that he provokes me with his sarcastic remarks, his criticisms. I feel that he's always putting me down. It hurts. I hate it. I suppose it would be better for me to blow up and get angry, but I refuse to give him that satisfaction. Besides, even if I did, I don't know whether he'd get the point. . . . The net result is I don't want to go to bed with him. It's a matter of pride, I guess. But it's more than that. How can I want to make love with him when I feel either tired and exhausted around him or hurt by his remarks?"

Because the person likely to experience depression has usually invested a great deal of feeling in, and dependency on, the object of his love, being rejected—losing the love and sexual interest of the person he loves—serves as one of the main triggers for activating or intensifying feelings of depression. This is as true of homosexual relationships as it is of heterosexual ones.

When the rejection is subtle, insidious, concealed, the individual may live in a state of chronic depression for years, unless and until an acute state of despair and upheaval terminates the malignant pattern. Jim Smith was thirty-five years old when he attacked and brutally beat his twenty-nine-year-old wife, Nancy. The police were called, and he was sent by ambulance, humiliated and confused, to the psychiatric unit of his local hospital. The marriage was destroyed beyond hope. Jim's image of himself as a reasonable, well-balanced person was shattered in the process.

Four weeks of treatment quieted his agitation and to some measure relieved his hopelessness. After his discharge, he arranged with his attorneys the details of the divorce settlement and left town to re-establish himself as a lawyer in another community.

Jim had been brought up in a conservative, middle-class home in the Midwest. He was an honors graduate from his state university and attended Yale Law School. Although he was an attractive and sociable young man, he felt somewhat shy with girls. His sexual experiences were quite limited. When Nancy, his wife-to-be, sought him out and aggressively pursued him, he was first flattered, then very turned on sexually, then, finally, trapped by the involvement and his sense of commitment to her—a commitment arising from genuine love, but also from a sense of responsibility for the first person with whom he thought he had shared sexual and emotional closeness.

Unfortunately, Nancy at twenty-two was incredibly naïve. She had many suitors, none of whom particularly interested her. She tended to regard men as a challenge. If they were interested in her, she rapidly lost interest in them. If they seemed aloof and uninterested, she felt compelled to seek them out and make new conquests.

Before she married Jim, her sexual and personal interest in him had already begun to evaporate. Several days before their marriage, she had actually dated and slept with one of her old boy friends, in what she regarded as a last gesture toward her gay single life, a farewell to fun and youth. Asking herself why she intended to go through with the marriage, her answer was: "He's attractive, stable, a good catch, and besides, I do love him in my own way. I'll make him a decent wife."

During the seven years of their marriage, prior to

its tragic climax, they had two children. After the birth of the first child, less than a year following their marriage, Nancy's lack of interest in sex became apparent to Jim. She and Jim never discussed it. Whenever he tried to bring up the subject, she managed to evade it. She felt that she did not want to hurt him by telling him she didn't want any more sexual contact with him. For a while he felt jealous, wondering if she was involved with someone else—a common reaction of one who is slightly depressed and feeling rejected. Gradually he became impotent, and then Nancy could point to the fact that the lack of sexual desire was mutual.

Jim's sense of self-esteem, though compromised, was nonetheless sufficiently reinforced by becoming a parent, having an attractive wife who was also a social asset, and progressing creditably in his law career. He could ignore the despair he felt whenever he thought of the lack of sexual and emotional intimacy in his marriage. Nancy could ignore that lack because she had never really experienced Jim in a close and loving way to begin with. She had never looked at him as a person, and so there was no way in which her initial infatuation with him could have developed into a relationship of love.

Then, after seven years of marriage, she met someone else who turned her on and was a challenge, as in the old days. This affair enabled her to be free of the fears she had felt on approaching her thirtieth birthday. She was "in love" again. She asked Jim for a divorce.

After six weeks of insomnia, of pleading with her to go with him for marriage counseling, of looking fruitlessly for an explanation for what had happened, Jim had too much to drink one evening. Dismissing the idea of suicide, which he had been seriously considering for several days, he cornered his wife and demanded that she stay with him. When she coldly refused, he struck her several times with his fist, becoming more enraged and frightened as she fell to the floor, bleeding, screaming. For a moment he thought of rushing to the window and jumping out. Instead, he reached for the telephone and called the police.

Throughout their marriage, Nancy had been curiously free of feeling any emotional dependency on Jim. Not wanting him sexually, and not loving him with any emotional depth, she was placed in a uniquely controlling position in the marriage. Jim, as a result, felt subliminally rejected and became increasingly more dependent on her. When she announced her intention to divorce him, it seemed to him as if his entire world were collapsing. He became acutely depressed, and might have succeeded in committing suicide had his hurt and rage toward her not been suddenly liberated.

Psychoanalytic theories stress that the depressed person's sensitivity to a loss of love is rooted in the way such a person loves. Specifically, he tends to become too involved, to place too much dependency on the person he loves, to lose too much of his identity in the relationship. If such a person should become involved with someone whose ability or willingness to give is considerably less than his own—as is often the case, unfortunately—a serious imbalance is set up. Unless the difference in the way of loving is understood by both and mutually accepted, the one who is more involved may frequently feel rejected, search frantically for evidence of affection, and intensify his anxiety over the possibility that the relationship may end. "He who loves the more," wrote Thomas Mann in *Tonio Kreuger*, "is inferior and must suffer. . . ."

Another important link between sexuality and depression is the guilt that is activated when sexual experiences cause a loss of personal integrity. Throughout the centuries, cultural values, moral teachings, and the conflicts and personality characteristics of many parents have combined to inculcate a high level of guilt about many kinds of sexual behavior. But in the last decade an extensive reconsideration of sexual values—in regard to many forms of activity ranging from masturbation to marital infidelity to homosexuality—has taken place. Some people are delighted by these changes; some are angered by them; most people find them confusing and upsetting. One father described a typically contemporary dilemma as follows: "This guy's been coming to the house on week ends, and he sleeps in my daughter's room. She's only sixteen. I can't get him out. It makes me see red. My wife is afraid that if we take a firm stand, my daughter will leave and end up living with him somewhere. When I suggested he use the guest room, he thought I was being funny and just laughed."

While a more open and honest attitude toward sex has been long overdue, the current sexual revolution has unfortunately obscured the healthy guilt that should attach itself to sexual activities liable to jeopardize a person's sense of worth. This kind of guilt is actually a protective device to help a person avoid sexual liaisons that might diminish his self-esteem and lead to depression. Without such protection, many people are more susceptible, in the face of so many sexual opportunities, to engaging in behavior that may be inappropriate, premature, and at times degrading. In the process of getting rid of—with good cause—the undesirable inhibitions and restrictions that made sex "dirty," the capacity of many people to recognize and cope with healthy sexual guilt has been lost as well.

Although the suppression of sexual guilt has become a widespread phenomenon—marital infidelity appears to be commonplace and has even been advocated by some as a palliative for an unsatisfactory marriage—this situation poses a special problem for the adolescent.

Peer pressure forces more and more youngsters to engage in sexual activity long before they are emotionally prepared for sex. The teen-ager has many tasks to accomplish, among them finding out who he is, defining the extent and limits of his own personality. He is naturally somewhat shy. Sex has been a mystery to him and traditionally an experience to be explored gradually, experimentally, so that it can eventually become integrated into his whole personality.

Working against this evolutionary pattern is the push of instant sex, a pressure so intense that he begins to feel that if he does not follow this lead, there must be something wrong with him. For young girls to be faced at fourteen with such issues as birth-control pills and abortions, when their sexual needs are still intimately interwoven with romantic ideals, can disrupt healthy personality development. Many teen-age boys are not ready for the complex emotional overtones that accompany full sexual activity. A certain amount of confusion, ennui, and even the extensive use of alcohol and drugs among teen-agers must be attributed to the pressure placed on them to involve themselves in sexual and emotional situations for which they are not prepared.

The roots of depression are found in how one regards oneself. Nowhere is mood more likely to be affected than in matters of love and sex. A fulfilling sexual relationship gives enormous reinforcement to one's sense of being whole and desirable, providing it occurs in the framework of mutual respect, trust, and caring.

9
Anger and Aggression

THE WORD "aggression" means, essentially, to move toward. It is a simple word of Latin origin that connotes energy and direction. In recent years especially, the word has acquired enormous moral and emotional overtones. A poll of one hundred college students on whether it conveyed a "good" or "bad" meaning resulted in an almost fifty-fifty split. Half the group interpreted it to mean the drive and force necessary to build, to accomplish constructive goals. To the other half it meant a destructiveness related to war, violence, exploitation.

Moral precepts that have influenced Western civilization—such as "the meek shall inherit the earth," "turn the other cheek," and "it is easier for a camel to go through the eye of a needle than for a rich man to enter the kingdom of God"—have infused into the cultural unconscious a certain amount of guilt over the process of taking decisive action to reach desired objectives. The blame cannot be placed so much on religious and moral teachings as on popular misinterpretations of these teachings. For example, it was in fact physically possible for a camel to pass through the Eye of the Needle; the Eye was a gate in the city of Jerusalem, and it was primarily a matter of law that forbade the passage of camels through it.

In contemporary society aggression has become synonymous with invading someone else's territory, whether militarily, as in Vietnam and Korea; financially, as in the invasion of another company's sales region; or personally, as in the exploitation of one human being by another. To call someone "aggressive" nowadays is to use the word as a pejorative label, implying that he is selfish, greedy, hostile, and at times dangerous. While it is true that the pursuit of one's goals may have a detrimental effect on someone else, it is more a matter of how and in what context aggression is mobilized.

Actually, aggressiveness can be considered a healthy and highly moral personality trait when directed toward legitimate goals and when the rights of the individual and the rights of others are properly balanced. The movement in education, for instance, toward a system that allows different pupils within the class to move ahead at different rates of learning speed, based on their inherent abilities, is a step toward a liberation of healthy aggression. Previously, the brighter student had been penalized, held back for the sake of the group, while the slower student was painfully aware of his slowness whenever he compared his grades with those of his classmates. The efforts of more progressive corporate groups to expand not so much by merger, acquisition, and the setting up of new divisions, but rather by establishing new small, innovative companies whose managers own a "piece of the action" and have a greater degree of independence, is a good example of releasing constructive aggression. There is also an opportunity for positive aggression in the student movement seeking access to curriculum committees and a share in the determination of the nature of their education.

Any individual's ability to be constructively aggressive is closely tied to his mood, emotional state, and personality. The libido theory of Freud posited that every human being possesses a given quantum of energy—biological energy derived from organic and genetic sources. The extent to which that energy is free to be utilized may be limited by many factors. Even when environmental opportunities for being aggressive are present—when initiative and creative action are valued and not smothered—the majority of people have an inner block limiting their freedom to be aggressive.

"Creative people are hard enough to find," said one experienced business entrepreneur. "Dependable people are even harder to find, and people with energy and follow-through, those who keep moving and see that the job gets done, are rare indeed. Our society doesn't seem to breed self-starters, and when initiative shows itself, everyone seems quick to chop it down."

Because the majority of men and women have some degree of inhibition in the free outward flow of energy, they are often frightened by demonstrations of initiative in others. Envy and competitiveness may also be activated. For every person who really takes pleasure in the achievements of others, there are many more who envy, resent, and criticize these achievements to compensate for their own lack of aggressiveness.

Because of the normal need for acceptance, a great many bright and capable individuals are discouraged from being aggressive and thus running the risk of social rejection. Everyone recalls the pressures within school to minimize academic performance and to deny any pleasure in the learning process simply to avoid being ridiculed and ostracized by classmates. Peer pressure perversely demands mediocrity.

In addition to environmental influences, the ability of an individual to be constructively aggressive depends on elements within his own personality. One of the most important is the freedom with which he can manage anger. Aggression is not the same as anger, but the ability to be aggressive is closely related to the success with which a person handles angry emotions.

The depressed individual is usually unable to experience and express normal anger. Instead, according to psychoanalytic theory, the anger is turned "inward against the self." Often the anger rumbles around disguised as tension, agitation, intestinal distress, fear —anything but what it really is. Walter B. Cannon, the physiologist, described what he called the fight-flight reaction: the human being, when confronted with danger, will react either with anger—self-defense or attack—or fear and, if possible, flight. For the depressed person, fear and/or flight is the usual way of responding to stress, even when in a normal mood anger would be the more appropriate response.

There are a number of reasons why people who are chronically depressed or depression-prone have a difficult time managing their angry feelings. Perhaps the most important is the fact that the way in which people handle emotions is a learned pattern, passed on from generation to generation within families and cultures. If, for example, expressing legitimate anger was simply not tolerated within the home and if any show of independence or defiance was firmly thwarted, emotions would be driven underground. Feelings would be concealed and communication stifled.

A case in point is a fifty-one-year-old woman who began to have insomnia and episodes of anxiety as she grew uncertain about her relationship to her husband, who throughout their marriage had offered little affection and support but ample criticism. He paid no heed to birthdays and anniversaries. He was abrupt with her whenever she disagreed with him even on minor points. He made all the major decisions in the marriage by himself.

For nineteen years she had collaborated with this pattern without complaint and supported him in many ways. Then, suddenly, her father died. During her period of grief, she began to question the quality of her married life. She had been hurt and angry on many occasions, but had ignored her feelings in the interest of harmony. The only way in which her feelings had expressed themselves was through a series of minor physical illnesses, which periodically disrupted their family and social life.

When she finally spoke up, as she emerged from her acute depressive reaction, her husband proved himself willing to work on his attitudes so as to demonstrate more warmth and a greater appreciation of her worth. "Over the years, it was almost as though she were inviting me to be indifferent," he complained. "Why didn't she speak up sooner?"

The answer was to be found in her own upbringing. Her parents, rigid and unemotional, had tolerated no disagreement within the home. Each was preoccupied with the role he played, that of husband or wife, mother or father, provider or housekeeper. Each role had certain expectations attached to it, and these were lived up to strictly and without complaint. Very little affection was shown, and never any anger. The children were discouraged from being spontaneous. They were rarely given any praise.

The inflexibility and emotional sterility of her home proved to be a breeding ground for her problems in experiencing and handling emotions, especially anger. As an adult, she concealed her sensitivity and lack of self-confidence. Unwittingly, her husband played into the pattern by neglecting her feelings, thereby reinforcing both her lack of emotional spontaneity and her doubts about her worth. Nor could she bring herself to tell him about her feelings, since doing so might liberate some of the anger she had suppressed.

After her father died, she became acutely depressed and sought counseling. In the course of her therapy, she began, for the first time, to ventilate some of the hurt and anger she had felt, and to reveal the pain of her compromised self-esteem. As her emotions were released, she showed not only a lifting of spirits but also a progressive increase in her level of energy. For the first time in years, she felt free to take the initiative in communicating with her husband. The anger she had been accumulating was now directed outwardly in her own defense. As this anger subsided, it was replaced by a greater freedom of expression. She was able to confront and deal with issues as they came up, either calmly and directly, or with anger if appropriate.

The discharge of hostility leading to a lifting in mood and a return of normal aggression is a pattern commonly seen in the therapy of the depressed person. It is as if there has been a storing up of unexpressed rage that is subsequently let out in bits and pieces until it has all been released. Psychoanalytic theory stresses that the depressed person tends to have a strong identification with the person he loves, at times so strong that the lines separating the two individuals become blurred. Hence to be angry at a parent or a lover is to be angry at oneself. When this anger is redirected outwardly, self-esteem can be restored.

Psychoanalytic theory would place the major causal factors for the depressed patient's fear of his own anger within the framework of childhood development, in particular at the oral and anal stages. In the former stage, traumatic events produce a great deal of difficulty in the way the individual later experiences dependency needs. When these needs are frustrated, in reality or in his imagination, his response is an unreasonable rage.

During the anal phase of development, when the child is approximately three years old, toilet training is completed. Too great a rigidity in child rearing at this time can serve to constrict the child's normal spontaneity and enthusiasm, devitalizing the youngster, shutting off his creative potential, introducing sadistic and masochistic components into his interpersonal relationships, and leading to a compulsiveness that denies him resilience in his later years. Such a combination of fixation points in childhood may produce an adult with intense unmet dependency needs, which are a source of frustration and anger, and a rigid inability to express emotions, referred to by Wilhelm Reich as an "affect block." This sets the person up for depression.

Freud himself postulated that biological factors would be identified and found to be closely linked to many of his psychological concepts, including those about the relationship between hostility and depression. It is now known, for example, that patients with hyperthyroidism (overactivity of the thyroid gland) tend to be exceedingly emotional, showing irritability and anger at the slightest provocation, while those with an underactive thyroid gland tend to be apathetic and depressed. The treatment of hyperthyroid patients, either surgically or by means of drugs that suppress thyroid overactivity, leads to a reduction in irritability and hypersensitivity. The correction of hypothyroidism, through the administration of thyroid hormones, reduces the apathy and restores the patient's ability to experience and express anger when provoked.

The strong connection between anger and depression and the concomitant block in spontaneity and aggressiveness are further intensified by the depressed person's sensitivity and low self-esteem. There are more opportunities for him to be hurt, offended, threatened —precisely because his sense of worth is already compromised. He often reads rejection into the slightest remark or indifference that ordinarily would not upset him. Paradoxically, the behavior of the depressed person frequently provokes anger and rejection from others, rather than the warmth he really seeks. Depression can be especially irritating to those in contact with a depressed person when the mood itself is an expression of his inner rage.

Harry Wright was associate dean of a small college in New England. He was thirty-eight years old when the dean retired. Harry, having done an excellent job for the school, had expected to be chosen as his successor. However, for various reasons the board of directors decided to look outside the school for a new dean. Harry did not receive the promotion.

He was deeply hurt. He felt, with good reason, unappreciated. This in turn set off a chain reaction in which he began to question his own ability and wonder whether or not he was good enough for the job. Perhaps he had overestimated his own abilities. He wondered whether he might have offended some key members of the college community. He was depressed.

Harry's anger, rather than being expressed in a direct and open manner, was repressed. Nonetheless, it surfaced in a "not caring" attitude. He no longer applied himself energetically to his work as he had. He was often late for faculty meetings or missed them completely. The new dean, only vaguely familiar with Harry's past contributions to the school, became irritated again and again by his indifference and reprimanded him for his irresponsibility. Harry felt even more unappreciated, since he failed to see the link between his behavior and the dean's impatience with him, and his hurt and anger doubled. When he was asked to resign, he was shocked and finally, when it was rather late, openly enraged by the situation.

Harry's disappointment at not receiving the deanship was quite understandable. However, his inability to initiate a discussion of his situation with the new dean, and the progressive accumulation of *anger in the form of depression,* prevented him from finding better solutions to the problem. He might have anticipated the possibility that the school would look elsewhere for a new dean. Inasmuch as he was well thought of, he might have communicated his interest in the position more definitively. Once the appointment had been made, if he felt the need to leave he might have handed in his resignation rather than forcing it by his behavior. He might also have continued to do his excellent work until the new dean was able to see and acknowledge his value to the school.

Because he could not handle his anger, Harry fell back on the use of depression to express his frustration and, in turn, received anger in response. This kind of pattern illustrates what is referred to as "passive-aggressive behavior," in which aggression, rather than being channeled actively and directly toward goals, is bot-

tled up, and the person sets out to make his point by a
circuitous route that permits him to disown—even to
himself—any responsibility for the outcome.

Indirect methods for expressing hostility are
learned. All children recognize that if they hurt themselves, their parents will react. As children find better
ways of eliciting a response, they gladly forfeit such
dramatic and self-defeating ways of getting attention or
expressing frustration. In the formative years of the
person likely to engage in passive-aggressive behavior,
one usually finds a serious confusion in communication
and a lack of responsiveness in the environment that
impresses on the child the idea that injuring himself
is the quickest and most effective way of "getting back
at" those who may have hurt him.

This can easily become a habit of failure. In adolescence, for instance, the somewhat depressed youngster may express disappointment and anger with his
parents by doing poorly in school. He cannot concentrate effectively. He consistently fails tests. He hands
his homework in late, and even then it is sloppy. In a
posture of failure, he brings home a report card that
makes his parents angry and frustrated. Any effort
on their part to force a change meets with stubborn
resistance.

The young underachiever is commonly depressed
and angry. His inadequate performance says to his
parents: "I am hurt. I am angry, but you haven't offered me a decent way of expressing my emotions."
The secretary who is repeatedly late for work and the
customer who is always several months late in paying
his bills in spite of having adequate cash on hand may

not be merely demonstrating a kind of carelessness. Frequently, this kind of behavior pattern is unconsciously designed to disturb its target and is an oblique way of expressing hostility. The intense immobilization of the seriously depressed individual is often itself an expression of passive rage.

Ethnic factors profoundly influence the manner in which an individual experiences and handles anger, and this is true in America even if the person is two or three generations removed from his origins. Not only are patterns for handling anger passed on, by contact, from generation to generation, but also, in the light of Jung's concept of the cultural unconscious, it would be naïve to assume that a few thousand miles and a century or so would significantly change the inherent architecture of the emotional life. In a society that is basically "a melting pot," there is no way to calculate the extent to which communication difficulties in a marriage are rooted in clashes of ethnic characteristics. In one instance, a husband and wife found that though they were highly compatible in almost every way, the difference in the way each handled anger nearly destroyed their marriage. The husband, whose father was Spanish, felt quite free to explode in rage at a minor slight. It was all over in a few minutes and he was then ready to completely forget the incident. His wife, who was of Scotch-English origin, valued control over emotions and did not like to get angry. When her feelings were hurt, she tended to become silent and withdrawn, feeling a strong sense of rejection and of futility stemming from her inability to discharge the emotions stirred up in her. When she retaliated, it was usually in the form of subtle, provocative remarks aimed at deflating her husband's ego. Until, in a counseling situation, they came to grips with this impasse, until he appreciated the full impact of his outbursts and she learned to be more self-expressive, their relationship was seriously jeopardized.

Transcultural studies document the fact that men and women brought up in strict religious settings, particularly if they are from families of North European origin, show a tendency toward withdrawal in the face of anger. Becoming depressed is a common way for them to respond to provocation. By contrast, those from less rigid religious backgrounds, particularly if they are of southern European origin, show the opposite tendency—less overt depression and more readiness to direct intense emotions outward when angered.

Just getting out anger is not necessarily therapeutic for all people who are depressed. At first, this may seem to contradict the concept that depression itself is frequently an expression of hostility and that the depressed person regains his energy and aggressiveness as he becomes more capable of emotional release. However, some of the anger the depressed person experiences comes from his hypersensitivity: his low self-esteem encourages him to feel rejected by others, whether he is or not. The hurt that he feels often derives as much from the way he perceives what is happening to him as from the actual facts of the matter.

If a certain amount of the anger the depressed person struggles with is the result of having been wounded, in fact or fancy, being able to express this hurt angrily will discharge some of his tension, but it will not automatically take away the underlying depression. In the individual who has had lifelong problems with hypersensitivity and has tightly controlled his hostile emotions, sudden outbursts of anger, which he might be encouraged to show in the course of an encounter session, can hardly be expected to change his ingrained pattern. In fact, such an experience may backfire, causing him to panic in the face of the overwhelming and unfamiliar emotions that have been aroused.

Not all depressed individuals suppress hostility. In some instances, anger and violence are as much the result of the depression as a cause. "I haven't been doing well in school," a sixteen-year-old boy said. "I can't concentrate on studies. I tried athletics, but couldn't make the team. At home, my mom is hell on wheels. She screams at me all the time. Uses lousy language. Calls me every four-letter name in the book. She's always after me, makes me feel like a nothing. No wonder Dad left her. There's no future for someone like me. Get some money. Get out of this place."

The boy just quoted was not from a slum but from an upper-middle-class suburban home. He had been arrested by the police for breaking into a hardware store, striking the salesman, and stealing some merchandise that he hoped to sell in order to get enough money to leave town. Abused at home, lacking a father with whom he could identify, unsupported by any kind of achievement in school or among his peers, he was indeed desperate. His hopelessness had led him to resort to a violent act in order to escape and, at the same time, discharge some of the rage he felt at his situation.

When individuals are out of touch with their emotions, and especially when they blame others for their distress, it is common for hostility, rather than being suppressed or repressed, to be very much on the surface, hiding the underlying depression.

Anne Richardson was going through menopause. She was physically comfortable, except for some hot flashes and lightheadedness from time to time. She had had difficulty in sleeping and ate poorly, but seemed to be in good spirits. No one suspected that she was depressed.

However, she was extremely difficult to live with. She incessantly found fault with her husband and children. If the house was untidy, she screamed until the newspapers were picked up and the ash trays emptied. When her husband would come home late from work, she nagged him about his negligence. He found it hard to pin her down in making plans for week ends, but when the time came for them to go away on trips or entertain friends, she would belabor him for not having made adequate plans.

There is such a thing as an "angry" depression. Anne Richardson differs little from the business executive whose depression shows itself as abruptness, irritability, impatience. At home he is short with his family and does not want to hear about day-to-day difficulties. At work he finds fault with minor failures on the part of his employees. He comes across as a constantly angry man. He may try alcohol or a brief affair as curative measures. He denies to himself that he is —or ever was—depressed. Denial of this sort is commonly associated with open and, at times, intense anger and the tendency to blame others for one's misfortunes.

It is important to realize, however, that not everyone who is depressed is necessarily angry, either consciously or unconsciously. There is such a thing as a direct and uncomplicated depressive response that may be set off by a disappointment, a rejection, or a loss. While depressed, such a person may not be able to activate his anger when provoked, but anger itself plays no significant role in the origins of the depression.

No discussion of hostility is complete without considering the nature of resentment. Resentment is different from anger. It is also different from depression. In fact, an acute depression can often save a hurt and disappointed person from the ravages of resentment.

Psychiatrist Oskar Diethelm and pharmacologist Joseph Reilly detected in their studies a biologically active substance unique in the blood of patients who were resentful. These investigators carefully defined resentment as a persistent and tenacious state of hostility, a "sustained feeling of bitterness about an injury, and a desire for revenge. . . . Inherent in resentment is the factor of projection and resulting suspiciousness." The resentful person feels a hatred and cynicism that he justifies by real or imagined hurts derived from his environment. Resentment is different from the repressed or suppressed hostility seen in certain psychoneurotic and depressed conditions, and is quite different from direct anger.

The resentful person lacks insight. He is usually insensitive to the feelings of others. He is likely to be unhappy primarily when he cannot dominate or control others in his environment, and especially when his demands cannot be immediately fulfilled. He cannot forgive slights and rejections, many of which are unintentional or entirely apocryphal, and he appears to derive pleasure from finding fault with the people around him.

Resolving resentment demands the adoption of a fresh value structure that allows the individual to let go of slights and forgive others. It is not an easy change to make. Whenever resentment is a major emotional factor in any psychological picture, whether an anxiety state, a depression, or even alcoholism, the prospects for recovery are seriously diminished. The resentful person is too busy thinking up ways of getting even, of making others suffer, of denying his own complicity in his unhappiness to become overtly depressed. He is, in fact, depressogenic; that is, he is likely to make others in his environment feel depressed if they are continually in contact with his bitterness.

By contrast, the depressed person often reveals a willingness to forgive, an eagerness to start anew as the depression lifts. His value structure emphasizes the importance of love, and this endures even when his mind is full of angry and desperate thoughts.

If aggressiveness has become a controversial characteristic in this culture, there is another characteristic equally as controversial and often ignored, one that is no less central to an understanding of depression in Western man: guilt.

10
Guilt

THE CULTURE in which a person lives shapes the way he experiences depression. In this regard, the major difference between cultures is the issue of guilt: who is to blame—even when no one is to blame—for the events causing the depression, and even for the depression itself.

Guilt, since it involves loss of self-esteem, can bring on depression, and the depressed person can feel guilty about being depressed. But these effects are unique to Western civilization. Transcultural psychiatrists have observed that certain signs of depression—insomnia with early morning awakening, social withdrawal, loss of interest in one's usual pursuits—are common to all cultures. In Western Europe and the United States, however, a loss of sexual interest and feelings

of guilt are common features of depression, in contrast
to many African countries where the element of guilt
is singularly lacking.

The African psychiatrist T. A. Lambo attributed
this difference to the specific nature of moral teachings
in Western culture in contrast to that of the African
countries. The American sociologist S. Kirson Wein-
berger ascribed it to two other factors: the differences
in child-rearing practices and the degree to which the
individual feels a sense of responsibility for what happens to him. In Kenya, for instance, the mother weans
her infant gradually and casually, and the child has
numerous maternal surrogates within the tribe. In
Western society, the bond between the mother and
child is more exclusive and much more intense. This
results in the infant's making a stronger identification
with the mother, both the "good" mother who loves
and the "bad" mother who deprives or becomes angry.
Such identification is a necessary step in the formation
of the superego, the self-ideal of which conscience is
a part. When the mother-child relationship is less intense, as in Kenya, the infant will not form as strong
a superego, and hence the propensity for guilt will be
less.

These child-rearing differences are reinforced by
value systems. In Europe and the United States there
is a strong emphasis on the individual's responsibility
for himself. When something goes wrong, it is natural
to assume that it is one's own doing. Even depression is
readily interpreted as a punishment.

On the other hand, the value system within many
African countries encourages people to project blame

onto other people or onto malevolent gods. When things go wrong, anger is directed outward, and when exposed to stresses that in Western man might provoke depression with guilt, the members of these cultures are much more likely to engage in violent and aggressive outbursts against real or presumed sources of their unhappiness. This type of reaction is reinforced by the great degree of group support within the tribe and the minimal emphasis on individual culpability.

Guilt, then, is a major factor in depression—both as a cause and as a consequence—in Western man. The results of guilt can be devastating.

Whenever she felt unhappy, Emily Watts feared that she would lose her husband's love. She would ask him, again and again, whether he cared for her. At first he was reassuring. Later, as the same question continually resurfaced, he became impatient. She in turn would only feel more frightened of losing him.

She had spasms of irrational jealousy, and would search her husband's suits and wallet for evidence that he might be involved with another woman. When he went on business trips, she could not sleep at night. She pressured him repeatedly to quit his job and find one that did not require traveling. It never occurred to her that her fears were rooted in guilt, that her feelings of being unattractive and inadequate as a wife were a form of self-punishment, that her ultimate punishment would be the loss of the man she loved.

Why did Emily feel a need to be punished, and in this way? This was her second marriage. She had become involved with her present husband while she was still married to her first. Her first marriage had been problematic from the beginning; at nineteen, she had run away from home and married a young man she hardly knew. He subsequently began to drink heavily, and several times, in an angry stupor, he beat her up. He was never able to hold a job for more than a few months, usually getting fired after an argument with a supervisor. But because of her conviction that marriage should be a permanent contract, she persisted for three years in trying to make it work.

When she began her affair, she experienced a great deal of guilt over it. As it went on, she suppressed her guilt, telling herself that she had a perfect right to find some kind of closeness and happiness. Six months after she left her first husband, he committed suicide. Emily was torn between knowing that she had not directly caused his death and feeling that if she had stayed with him longer he might still be alive.

She did not call her feeling guilt. Yet she did feel intensely responsible for what had happened to him. She told no one of her conflict. Gradually she became depressed and developed the fear that her new husband, with whom she had been very happy, would eventually leave her.

In the course of professional counseling, Emily Watts saw for the first time the connection between her depression and the fear and guilt she had felt during her first marriage. "I thought that the best thing to do was to try to push it all out of my mind. I never talked about what happened to anyone. I can see I was wrong. It never occurred to me that I would feel so terribly responsible for something I had so little control over."

Even when feelings of guilt are not the cause of depression, guilt is easily provoked when someone is feeling despondent. A thirty-two-year-old foreman lost his job suddenly, and a few months later his wife deserted him. His assumption—an unwarranted one—was that he had caused both these misfortunes. "If I had only treated her differently, she wouldn't have left me. And my job—if only I'd put in extra hours, they wouldn't have let me go." The fact was that his wife had never loved him. She had married him on the rebound from a love affair in which she had been rejected, and had found him lacking in what she "expected of a husband" from the earliest days of their marriage. As for his job, his employers had dismissed him only because they had lost several important contracts and could no longer afford to keep him on the payroll.

Unable to gain perspective on either event, he persisted in blaming himself. At times, his vulnerability to feeling guilty went beyond reasonable limits. "Last week, at the new job, someone stole fifty dollars from one of the lockers. I know it's crazy, but when the company police started looking into it, I felt as if I had done it. When I got rid of that weird idea, I thought I would be accused of it anyway."

Psychoanalytic theory points to a powerful superego as part of the personality structure of the individual who becomes depressed. Formed in childhood, the superego has two major components. The first is a sense of right and wrong, commonly called conscience. When conscience is violated, when the individual feels that he has transgressed his basic values—or someone else's values he thinks should be his—the result is guilt.

The second component is self-ideal. When someone feels that he is pretty much the kind of person he wants to be, he can be reasonably content. The greater the distance between what he is and what he feels he ought to be, the greater his sense of failure. At times, the superego can be so highly developed that the standards the person expects to meet are impossibly high.

The superego is not the same as conscience; the former contains a strong emotional element, while the latter is a more intellectual awareness of one's value system. W. H. Auden, defining this difference in his book *A Certain World*, wrote:

> The superego speaks loudly and either in imperatives or interjections—"DO THIS! DON'T DO THAT! BRAVO! YOU SON OF A BITCH!" Conscience speaks softly and in the interrogative—"Do you really think so?" "Is that really true?"
>
> To say that their voices are different does not mean, of course, that they never coincide; indeed in a perfect society they would always coincide. . . .
>
> . . . The limitation of the superego as a guide to conduct is that, since it is a social creation, it is only effective so long as social conditions remain unchanged; if they change, it doesn't know what to say. At home, the Spartans did not use money; consequently, when they travelled to countries that did, they were helpless to resist the temptations of money, and it was said in the ancient world that a Spartan could always be bribed.

Unlike the Spartan away from home, the depressed person has a tendency to feel guilty, which makes him particularly vulnerable to those who know how to control him by activating his guilt. Because he often suffers from the assumption that he is somehow in the wrong, he is easily convinced that he is at fault in any situation, regardless of the facts.

A thirty-nine-year-old woman consulted a psychiatrist because she had been feeling hopeless and suicidal off and on for several months. "My husband said there was something wrong with me. We have terrible fights. He told me I was wrecking our marriage and if I didn't straighten out he'd have to leave me."

Over the next few sessions the following impression of her husband emerged: rigid, opinionated, a man who demanded a high level of performance from himself and who was unceasingly critical of his wife. At one time or another he accused her of not being a competent housekeeper, of failing to discipline the children adequately, of not entertaining enough, of being uninterested in him sexually. When she would become upset and cry, he would accuse her of being emotionally unstable. "Is he right? Am I a complete failure? Am I all these awful things he says I am?"

The psychiatrist insisted on meeting her husband to get a clearer picture of the interaction. During the entire visit her husband acted more as though he were a colleague of the doctor's rather than the husband of the patient. "What can we do for her, doctor? She's too sensitive. Of course I think highly of her—I love her. She really seems very depressed. Do you think she's seriously ill? There's a history of mental illness in her family, you know. Or perhaps she didn't tell you." He denied that he had done or said anything that could have been upsetting to her. "There's nothing wrong with me. I don't have to come to see you or anyone else." And he declined to make another appointment.

Within two months, the patient reported that her husband was now angrily complaining about the time consumed by her therapy. He had also claimed that he was in regular contact with her therapist for "progress reports," which he was not. He dropped remarks like, "Your doctor told me you're not doing enough to help yourself." His antagonism to her treatment appeared just as the patient herself was recovering some of her self-esteem and becoming better able to fend off his criticism of her.

The guilt-maker is not always so blatant in such efforts to make a husband, a wife, parent, child, or co-worker feel dreadful about himself or herself. Frequently the interaction occurs in a much tamer fashion. "Look how unhappy you are making your mother feel," and "Why can't you be more grateful for all we've done for you?" and similar remarks made at the right moment, in the right tone of voice and with the right nonverbal backup, are often enough to keep the slightly depressed person subject to the will and control of the guilt-maker. Such maneuvering can sometimes be so subtle that some therapists have resorted to videotaping families to show them the destructive quality in their communication patterns.

What motivates the guilt-maker? Most of the time he is totally unaware of his effect on others, since the motivation for that effect is buried too many layers below his awareness. Sometimes the guilt-maker is sadistic, deriving a certain amount of pleasure from making his victim squirm. Sometimes making others feel guilty is a way of discharging his own guilt, which may originate from problems into which he has little or no insight. Finding someone else to blame relieves him temporarily of his own tension and distress. Sometimes his behavior is rooted in envy and competitiveness: by making the other person feel incompetent and guilty, he can then feel more capable himself.

The guilt-maker rarely comes to the therapist's office, except to vindicate himself. As a rule he has too little insight. As long as he has someone to blame and control, he can protect himself more or less effectively against experiencing depression. It is his victim who often ends up depressed, feeling "I can never do anything right," and "It's all my fault."

Guilt, of and by itself, is not abnormal even when it leads to depression. The ability to experience and recognize appropriate guilt and the cultivation of effective ways of coping with guilt have always been considered necessary attributes of the healthy personality. Guilt is an important mechanism for protecting a person against becoming involved in behavior that is injurious to himself or others. When guilt is denied, or when the individual cannot recognize it or does not know what he ought to feel guilty about, he is likely to enter into situations that compromise his self-esteem. He may not realize how much he is hurting himself until he becomes acutely depressed. Linking his depression to his guilt and then finding a way of resolving the guilt are fundamental parts of his recovery.

"I've lost my enthusiasm for everything," said a forty-six-year-old salesman. "For the past two years nothing has worked out right. I put off making calls and I've lost customers as a result. On week ends when I'm home, I'm too tired to spend any time with the kids. My wife and I hardly talk to each other. When we do, it often ends up in a fight." As he explored the sources of his unhappiness in therapy, he revealed that he had been having an affair with the secretary of one of his customers for nearly two years. "That couldn't be getting me down. As a matter of fact, it's the one pleasure I have, getting into bed with her once or twice a month. Besides, what's so unusual about that? Everyone plays around."

It took several months before he could convince himself that, regardless of what others did or did not do, for him the sexual involvement was stirring up guilt. His behavior contrasted with his upbringing. He had attended religious schools as a child and, until his early twenties, had been deeply involved in church activities. He had not had intercourse with anyone before marrying his wife.

He had abided by the strict, demanding codes of his fundamentalist background until other demands in his life, particularly in business, forced him to make compromises. He began whittling away at his ingrained values. He took a drink from time to time. He arranged for occasional kickbacks. He padded his expense account here and there. "Everyone's doing it. If you don't you can't survive." He ignored occasional twinges of guilt. By the time he was in his middle thirties he looked on religion as "a real handicap to making it." Until he began his affair, his home life had been relatively placid. After that, largely as a product of his unrecognized guilt, he turned it into a battleground.

"Just what do I do with this guilt now that I recognize it?" he asked. "I'm certainly not going back to the way I thought twenty years ago." He was confronted with two options: either to modify his value system as far as fidelity in marriage was concerned or end his affair and try to improve his life at home. He chose to end the affair. But it was not an easy choice to make. He was incredulous that, surrounded as he was by sexual permissiveness, he could still feel more comfortable with his original set of values.

It is clear that this culture is replete with confusing and contradictory values. Consider the reactions to the recent decision of the Supreme Court on the legality of abortion. There are those who hold that life begins at the moment of conception and that abortion is murder. Others feel that there are good medical and psychological reasons to perform abortions selectively. Still others feel that male legislators have no right to determine arbitrarily what a woman can or cannot do with her own body. Certain groups insist that all hospital facilities should be made available for abortion procedures even if owned and operated by religious groups opposed to abortion.

Everything that has brought cultures and people into more immediate contact with one another—from television to jet planes—confronts the individual with a mass of available and contradictory options in the way of values. As a result it becomes difficult to know what to feel guilty about. This in turn leads to a Novocain effect—a numbing of one's personal sense of responsibility.

What a contrast to the world of Freud! The early

analysts worked out their theories in a period of relatively static values. They were able to study individuals
against the background of stable environmental influences. They could "cure" a patient by releasing his
ego from the constrictions placed on it by a stern and
severe superego, without throwing him out into a
world like ours, which does not differentiate between
neurotic guilt and real guilt, and which cannot distinguish the self-actualizing person from the psychopath.

"There is something seriously immobilizing in this
society," commented a university president. "Between
the blurring of values on the one hand and the mas-
sive bureaucracies on the other, you have to be psychopathic at times to get anything done. Otherwise,
you just get frustrated and bogged down."

The traditional psychopath is unconcerned with
the needs or rights of others. He seeks his own ends
exclusively, often by exploiting and using people. He
is unfamiliar with feelings of guilt. The vice-president
of a large film production company, in an effort to be
humorous, told the following story to his wife's psychiatrist, whom he visited only after she had made a
serious suicide attempt.

"We were in Los Angeles for a couple of days, a
business trip, contracts to take care of. Wanted to show
some of our customers a good time. Got this girl,
pretty, blond, mentally retarded. Promised a part in one
of our pictures if she'd give us a gang bang. So she did,
one after another. It was really something—and was
she surprised afterward when we told her to get lost!"

This executive was psychopathic. In everyday life
he was seen as a dynamic, energetic, and clever busi-

nessman who knew how to make money. To have the psychopath as a cultural hero is—to say the least—confusing. Millions of people have lost the sense of guilt and along with it the normal protective function that guilt serves. Often they can regain it only when an acute depression forces them to come to terms with their suppression of conscience.

There is a difference between depressed states that stem from guilt and those that are unrelated to feelings of guilt. Psychiatrist Peter F. Regan III demonstrated that depressed patients with a significant degree of guilt do not respond well to biological treatment. By contrast, depressed patients in whom guilt is not significant usually improve rapidly when biological treatments are used. Guilt will reinforce the tenacity of depression. It often propels the person to go on repeating the behavior pattern engendering the guilt until he has come to terms with it.

Certain depressed alcoholics exemplify this point. A fifty-one-year-old woman began therapy because of loneliness and feelings of despair that had plagued her for the two years subsequent to her husband's untimely death. She had also been using alcohol to take the edge off her depression, and had formed a habit of drinking nearly a fifth of Scotch every day.

Efforts on her own and through Alcoholics Anonymous to end her drinking proved unsuccessful. In fact, the more she focused on her drinking problem, the guiltier she felt and the more she drank. Through psychotherapy and with the aid of antidepressant medication, her depression gradually lifted. But her drinking continued until she was able to see how the anguish of the guilt itself was setting her up to drink again. Once she had forfeited her tendency to blame herself, she discovered a greater degree of inner freedom to control and eventually eliminate the drinking altogether.

Guilt is not always coexistent with depression, but it strongly determines the quality of the depression when it is present. For many, coping with depression means putting themselves back in touch with legitimate feelings of guilt.

There is also an urgent need for our society to clarify basic values by which its members can live. At a 1964 conference on Moral Values in Psychoanalysis, Roland B. Gittelsohn, who was then rabbi of Temple Israel in Boston, stated: "In physical medicine, the doctor treating the patient recognizes that there are certain physical laws of nature, such as the laws involving nutrition and exercise. While he knows that they are relative in the sense of being applied to the specific patient and the specific situation—that they will not apply precisely the same way to every individual—he also knows that these laws or rules are absolute.

"Isn't the same thing true of moral values? Are there not certain moral values and laws within a culture in conformity to which alone true health and happiness are possible?"

11
Success
Is
a
Risk

DEPRESSION has often been referred to as an "illness of success." It is frequently at the very point when the physician has established his successful practice, the businessman becomes executive vice-president of his company, the inventor finally wins his patent suit, that their lives do a somersault and depression sweeps in.

The Peter Principle maintains that many people are promoted one step beyond their capacity, after which they stabilize at that level of incompetence. There is an alternative to this concept. Promotion can bring on a depression, and the depression then passes for ineffectiveness. When a person attains the very goals he has been seeking, the risk of his becoming depressed rises sharply.

Success often brings major changes—social, economic, and sometimes geographic—plus greater responsibilities and pressures. Many individuals, because of a deeply rooted sense of guilt, feel unconsciously that they do not deserve what they have achieved, and turn about to undermine and destroy it. For everyone, the attainment of a major goal in life activates a reassessment of personal worth and direction.

In an "upward mobile society," as the sociologists call this one, being successful and having some external evidence of one's worth is a vital need. It is closely tied to self-esteem. Whether the goal consists of a higher position in a corporation, a larger income, the completion of a thesis or book, becoming a proficient athlete or winning a political contest, there is always a reinforcement of self-esteem in the achievement, and some degree of self-recrimination in not making it.

Paradoxically, the more dependent a person's view of himself is on external evidence of accomplishment, the less satisfying such achievements will be. An ambitious research scientist described his struggle with ambition in this way. "From the time I was a small child, I felt driven to do well. My parents pushed me in school. If I didn't get straight A's in everything, I felt frightened, hopeless, even at ten or eleven. I graduated from college *summa cum laude*. You'd think that would be enough to quiet my self-doubts. But not at all. I wondered whether I would do well in graduate school. I was concerned about whether I would do any research that would be worth doing. And even when I was given one of the highest honors in science thirty years later, I felt that I didn't really deserve it, that the work for which I was being given such recognition was something I had fallen into accidentally."

Even though the "I" within each of us defies measurement, most people search in one place or another for ways to translate self-worth into inches, yards, and feet. Every society has its own measuring stick. Using money as a guide to determine personal worth is a traditional one. In his *Anatomy of Melancholy* (1621) Robert Burton wrote: "In a word, every man for his own ends. Our *summum bonum* is commodity, and the goddess we adore *Dea Moneta*, Queen Money, to whom we daily offer sacrifices, which steers our hearts, hands, affections, all: that most powerful goddess, by whom we are reared, depressed, elevated, esteemed, the sole commandress of our actions, for which we pray, run, ride, go, come, labor and contend as fishes do for a crumb that falleth into the water. It is not worth, virtue, wisdom, valour, learning, honesty, religion or any sufficiency for which we are respected but money, greatness, office, honour, authority."

The close relationship in our culture between money and self-esteem is only too evident. It is not uncommon for people to have a sense of well-being only when a certain amount of cash is in their savings account. It is possible to watch the moods of certain individuals fluctuate with the ups and downs of the securities market. Because personal financial problems are often so real and immediate, it is often difficult in therapy to point out the powerful emotional element the person has introduced into his perception of money, even though it has little to do with the facts of the case.

Many successful men and women have been able to confirm themselves in their work—not through a confirmation of self-worth, but rather through a confirmation of talent and ability. A close look at the evolution of their lives shows a logical relationship between what they are doing now and the interests and natural inclinations they demonstrated in childhood and adolescence. A very successful businessman who thrives on his responsibilities recalled organizing a group of youngsters in high school to provide a service of doing chores around people's homes. He served as the agent and took a fee for locating the job and the worker and putting the two together. Thirty years later he was skillfully doing the same type of work for a computer programming company he had organized. A well-known writer recalled that his urge to write could be traced back as early as seven, when he created his own drawings for children's books, and again at nine, when he published a neighborhood newspaper that he typed, duplicated, and sold from house to house.

Obviously, there are many practical reasons that prevent people from doing the kind of work for which they are best suited. However, when a person *does* have some choice, if he loses sight of the importance of pursuing interests in harmony with his personality he runs a risk of forfeiting fulfillment. There are also forceful, though subtle, social pressures which cause discontent even in those who have found a satisfying place for themselves. A fifty-two-year-old housewife who came to therapy because of depression found herself unreasonably angry at what she felt was abuse from her family. "All day long it's my job to see that the house is clean, the meals are cooked, the dishes are done. From time to time my husband helps me. But he's gone most of the day. . . . I don't have much of an education. I was an average student in high school. I worked as a secretary for several years before I married. I didn't really enjoy that although it was nice having the extra money. If I went to work now, what I earned would be taxed on top of my husband's salary, but I feel that if I don't go to work, I'm losing out on something."

In the course of her therapy it became apparent that she had never had any special career interests. In fact, as a child and teen-ager she had always daydreamed of having a home of her own, of a husband and children. Her dreams were quite elaborate and detailed: collecting recipes, making covers for the couch and chairs, baking, tending to flowers in her garden, sitting down after dinner in the evenings sharing with her family their activities of the day. "That's what I always wanted. Now that I have it, why don't I enjoy it?"

Slowly and insidiously over the years she had become conditioned to believe that housework was demeaning, that there was something wrong with her if she admitted to herself that she enjoyed the day-to-day activities of being a wife and mother and had absolutely no desire to return to the world of business.

People commonly exchange their real feelings for feelings they are supposed to have. A successful physician complained that at the end of every day he arrived home in a state of exhaustion, barely able to participate in family life or recreation. "It's the terrible pressure I work under. I spend all day with patients, from eight A.M. until seven in the evening. You can't carry the weight of responsibilities I do and expect to be cheerful and energetic at the end of the day. And there's no way I can cut back."

There were two basic fallacies in this patient's thinking. The first was that as a physician he could not refuse to take patients referred to him, even though he might have referred them to other doctors when he was too busy. The second was his concept of work—that it was supposed to be hard and in some way unpleasant. Moreover, he had lost his own identity as a person in the role he had assumed as a physician. Envisioning the ideal doctor as conservative, thoughtful, quiet, and undemonstrative, he had thwarted even in his personal life his own tendency to be cheerful, spontaneous, humorous, and emotional in order to fit the image. As he began to realize, in therapy, that he really enjoyed his work and liked his patients, that he could see his life as a continuum rather than sharply divided into compartments, and that he did not have to hide himself behind a mask of formality at all times, his energy level increased. The days passed more quickly, and he was no longer so tired in the evenings. He had unlabeled himself and his life experiences, no longer calling them "work" and "play," and found that he could move from moment to moment without the extra burden of subconsciously defining each moment in terms of its appropriate category.

Many people who have achieved success have done so at a price, sacrificing something of value—family relationships and friendships, for instance—along the way. Once they have reached the goals they have set for themselves, they may suddenly become painfully aware of what they have missed. The depression they experience can afford them a chance to restore balance to their lives.

Richard Laszlo was forty-nine when he became depressed. An outstanding commercial designer, the creator of prize-winning automobiles, soda-pop bottles, and typewriter cases, he gradually, over a six-month period, lost interest in his work. He put things off, withdrew, and avoided social engagements. He had two important projects he could not begin. "I can't get going," he complained. "In spite of everything, I'm a failure."

From his early teens he had demonstrated a special talent in art and had applied himself intensively to its development. He found a great deal of gratification in his work. As he became more recognized, he began to feel alienated from his parents and brothers. His father, a clerk in a grocery store, and his mother, a secretary, had encouraged him to go to art school and wanted him to be successful. After he started moving in more sophisticated circles, he began to feel embarrassed about their manners and appearance, hating himself at the same time for his embarrassment. When he won an important art prize, he waited to invite them to the presentation until the last minute; feeling unwanted, they declined to come.

Richard also discovered that in spite of his success, he was not getting what he hoped success would bring—popularity and friendship. Because of his dedication to work in high school and college, and the fact that he had to work part-time to pay his expenses, he had led a somewhat isolated existence. He was lonely, but rarely thought about his loneliness. Moreover, he felt that he was different from many of the youngsters in school. "I was ambitious. Most of them seemed to be willing to settle for a lot less in life than I was. I wasn't disliked, but then I wasn't liked either. I figured that one day, when I made it, I'd have plenty of friends."

His success did bring many people into his world, but rather than caring about him as a person, most of them, as he sadly realized, were there to use him. For some he meant money. For others he meant contact with a celebrity. He did not know how to form close personal relationships; even when he married, he selected a woman who had been drawn to him not as a person, but by her image of him as a talented and prominent artist. The marriage reduced itself to arguments and jealousies; it lasted only four years and was childless. The loneliness that Richard had suppressed in his teens now swept in on him in full force. His basic human need for closeness had not, and could not, be fulfilled through his achievements. The success that had separated him from his parents, now aging, filled him with guilt. He felt betrayed by his own efforts. "I'm really a failure. I wish sometimes that I had never had any talent. It has cost me too much."

One of the elements that make success so costly is the highly competitive climate that surrounds the successful individual. It encourages loneliness and makes it difficult for him to find anyone with whom he can share his problems. A sales executive described his predicament in these terms: "When I was having a lot of difficulty at home—my wife was unhappy and we used to have one argument after another ending in threats of divorce—there just wasn't anyone I could talk to. At work I had what I would call working friends, but I couldn't open up to them. We had a veneer of camaraderie, but under the surface there was always the jockeying for better position. Besides, in business you're not supposed to have problems. Everyone does—but if you admit it or show it, you get tagged as unstable. It's a competitive ploy. . . . And having no one to share feelings with, everything became magnified in my mind. I couldn't get rid of things that kept bothering me or get any perspective. I just kept feeling more and more hopeless about things at home, and about my life in general."

Success is likely to stir up a kind of sadness because the achievement of a goal almost always involves an ending. Graduation from school, for most people a point of completion, commonly evokes a sense of loss. Finding the "right" man or woman and marrying, sending the last child off to school, finishing a project all convey at one and the same time a point of success and an ending. The feeling "It is over" and the question "Where do I go from here?" combine to activate depression and a reconsideration of self-worth.

When Edith Green married at twenty-two, she knew that Henry had no money and that they would have to live simply. She was quite prepared to put up with some deprivations while he finished his graduate work in architecture. They delayed having children for three years, while she worked as a secretary at the university. After graduation he obtained a good position with a large firm in New York. A year later their first child was born.

Young architects are not well paid, so Edith took a

part-time job as a bookkeeper. They lived in a one-bedroom apartment, and the baby slept in the living room. "This won't go on forever," she thought; "in a few years we'll be ready to enjoy life." In the summer they went to Jones Beach; in the winter they would share a bottle of chianti and pizza with friends. Occasionally they visited her parents in Florida. They went to the movies twice a month; otherwise, they usually watched television or played chess in the evening. Edith and Henry were "waiting."

On his thirty-ninth birthday, Henry was made a partner. His work had become well recognized. At forty thousand dollars a year, it was time for Edith and Henry and their two children, both in school, to move out of the city to a suburb.

Within a few months after moving to their new home, Edith began to experience a great deal of fear of going out of the house. She slept poorly at night. She was reluctant to meet any new people in the neighborhood. She put off decorating. Edith and Henry began to argue frequently, about nothing important. "What's happening?" she asked herself, worried and frightened.

For the first time, Edith Green was faced with the necessity of living with herself and her family without the preoccupation of not having enough money, enough room, enough time. A whole segment of her life was over and with it went the many pleasures she and Henry had shared, unnoticed since their joint focus had been on the "day when we make it." The moment they had both looked forward to for fifteen years had come, and neither of them was prepared for it. Depression, as it often does, deadened Edith's sense of enthusiasm as well as her sexual interest in Henry, and she began to wonder if she really loved him. It was a question she hadn't asked herself for years. Was she a good mother? Could she meet the social demands of their new neighbors? Would her children be able to adapt to the change in schools? Now that there was no longer any need for her to change diapers or rush off to her bookkeeping job or provide a young architect with encouragement, there seemed to be no need for her at all.

The Wall Street Journal recently referred to the wives of successful executives as the victims of success and documented the high incidence of alcoholism among these women. The children of families caught in the dilemma of a depressed mood accompanying success often openly rebel, rejecting the model of hard work and achievement they have been offered in favor of dropping out to "do their own thing." "I can't bear the guilt for my parents' unhappiness," said one adolescent girl. "Mother drinks too much and Dad is tired and irritable whenever he's home. He travels a lot. I've tried to speak with them, but they just won't listen. They have everything they ever seemed to want—a beautiful house I don't care if I never see again, their club, their friends. Dad's a top executive with an automobile company. But all their work hasn't made them happy. I think they were happier when they didn't have so much. They don't seem able to face themselves. I know it's not my fault, but I feel it is, somehow. That's why I can't afford to think about it any more. I don't know what kind of life I want, but I certainly don't want theirs!"

In the process of questioning the status symbols of

society and the competitiveness in which their parents
have immersed themselves, many young people, themselves floundering in search of goals, have rejected
those of their parents and have forced them to reconsider the definition of success. Describing such a confrontation with his twenty-year-old son, a depressed
business executive made this comment: "At first I was
angry at him about his attitudes toward school. He
was almost arrogant about what he thought should be
taught and what shouldn't be taught, instead of realizing that teachers with a lot more experience than he
had were making those decisions. But all my anger
did was to make things worse. He just stopped talking with me about his ideas. I had wanted him to
go into a profession, law or medicine. He kept throwing out all kinds of crazy ideas. He wanted to be a chef
one day, run a farm the next. The more I tried to
straighten him out, the more difficult he became. Finally I gave up trying. It was as if his refusal to listen
to me implied that I was a failure, as if all the efforts I
had made to become something—my father was a man-
ual laborer—had been for nothing."

Whether it is set off by conflicts with children or
by some other event, depression commonly occurs at
the point at which a person has reached the goals
toward which he has been striving. It is then that he
must reconsider who he is, what his life is about, and
where he will go from there.

12
Dependency, a Delicate Balance

THE FEELING OF HELPLESSNESS that accompanies depression is frightening. In severe moments of depression, a person may not be able to carry out ordinary tasks that could normally be done with ease. One woman, leaving her divorce lawyer's office, had to ask his secretary to accompany her to a subway she had been riding for ten years. A high school teacher with years of experience found that he could not prepare his lectures or correct quizzes because his concentration was so impaired.

Helplessness deepens a depressed mood, often forcing the person to become very dependent on those around him. Needing replaces wanting. The businessman who in better spirits felt that he had many options open to him should his job become unsatisfactory now feels, being depressed, that if he loses it, he could never find another one. A depressed young woman is convinced that her current boy friend is the only one who will ever fulfill her romantic expectations, and dreads the possibility of his rejecting her.

One of the reasons why depression increases feelings of helplessness and dependency is the frequent damming up of anger and rage. The more dependent the person becomes, the angrier he becomes under the surface as he struggles against his helplessness. Since he has trouble liberating his anger and being aggressive, the mounting rage intensifies his helplessness. Psychiatrists often observe a progressive increase in energy and self-confidence among depressed patients as anger is expressed and aggression released. "I started out in therapy unable to do anything," said one patient. "I couldn't concentrate. I couldn't communicate my ideas effectively. I couldn't get anything done. Over a period of weeks this formless rage came out in bits and pieces. I would clench my fists and pound on the arms of the chair. Every time I went through this, I felt more and more freed from an inner constriction, and more self-confident."

Feelings of helplessness are easily activated when dependency needs are especially strong. This is often a basis for depression. A common trigger for depression is loss. The more deeply dependent the individual has been on the person or things lost, the more depressed he will become.

In more intense dependency situations, there can actually be a blurring of the lines separating the two people involved. Such an interdependency is natural in infancy, when the three-month-old baby has yet to distinguish between himself and his mother as independent entities. A certain vestige of this confusion remains in most people, and may be reactivated in the experience of love. "I cannot live without you" may be a token of the depth and sincerity of the feeling one person has for another; or it may be meant literally, in the sense that the ego strength of one requires the constant love and approval of the other. It is as if there is something lacking in the personality that can be complete only when another person provides the missing ego link.

The vulnerability of the person whose sense of self depends on someone else is at once apparent. In order to maintain that relationship he will often go to great lengths, subjugating himself to all sorts of abuse and controlling behavior on the part of the person on whom he is dependent, in return for the security of thinking that the other person will "always be there." And if that person withdraws or rejects him, it is not just the loss of a close and meaningful relationship he must deal with, but the disruption of a system that has become essential for maintaining his sense of identity and wholeness.

"I was really hung up on Peter," said one young woman. "When I was with him I felt great. The rest of my life had meaning only because of him. When he would go away on a business trip or to visit a relative, I felt lost, lonely. I knew he loved me. But I needed constant reassurance of his love. I couldn't sleep. I ached all over. I was terrified that one day he might leave me.

"And one day he did. Not suddenly. He just kind of moved farther and farther away from me. I felt a terrible despair. I was convinced I would never find anybody else I could love that way. I needed him. I couldn't go on living without him. One night, after he abruptly hung up on me on the phone, I took an overdose. Without Peter, I was nothing, no one."

The kind of dependency that involves a loss of self is extreme. The average person is to varying degrees dependent on people and things in his world. How he will handle his dependency needs is determined in childhood. Erik Erikson emphasizes that one of the first qualities the child must develop in relation to his environment is trust—a trust born out of predictability. It is based on the clarity of the messages, verbal and nonverbal, delivered to him from his family. A great deal of insecurity in the infant's environment, particularly when that insecurity is rooted in anxiety and ambivalence toward him by his mother, creates a core feeling that "nothing and no one can ever really be trusted."

Such a lack of trust breeds serious difficulties that affect normal dependency needs. Instead of being able to allow himself to need another and still set limits on that need, the adult who emerges from such an environment will usually veer to one extreme or the other, either searching for the unattainable complete fulfillment of the dependency needs that were not met or rejecting any and all opportunities for healthy dependency, adopting a philosophy that "everyone must stand on his own two feet at all times."

Martin Shreiner was forty-nine when he had his

first heart attack. Until then he had always been a stubbornly energetic man. As sales manager for a large manufacturing company he often worked nights and week ends, and traveled extensively to see customers. It never occurred to him to delegate significant responsibilities to any of his key assistants, most of whom were eminently reliable. "If I don't do it myself," he maintained, "it never gets done right."

His physician advised him to make certain changes in his way of handling things if he wanted to remain in good health. In particular, Martin was told to set aside some time to rest each day, and rely on others in his department to perform the tasks that did not require his judgment or experience. Because of his unrecognized fear and deep reluctance to depend on anyone other than himself, he denied the relevance of the doctor's recommendations. Within a year he was hospitalized for a second coronary.

The ability to accept some degree of dependency determines the extent to which a person can accept and deal with physical illness as well as with emotional problems. A person who has a vested interest in denying the presence of ordinary dependency needs is especially threatened when he cannot influence and control circumstances around him. When such a person becomes depressed, the feelings of helplessness can snowball. The initial slowing up and concentration impairment may not in itself be severe, but his reaction to not being able to stay in charge of himself and his feeling that he is losing control can rapidly aggravate the depressed mood; at times it can reach panic proportions.

Many people are confused about the concept of independence, believing that it implies complete freedom from any dependency needs. Genuine self-reliance requires a reasonable appreciation of the fact that no matter how effective and self-confident a person is, there are going to be times and situations when he must depend on someone else. An excessive need for independence prevents many people from reaching out for professional or personal guidance when they need it.

Alice Donnard was so afraid of being dependent on others that when, at her husband's insistence, she made her first visit to a therapist, she could not sit down for more than five minutes at a time. "I think better when I'm standing," she said. "I like to walk around when I'm talking." She insisted on leaving the interview before her time was up and informed the therapist that she would have to call him to make another appointment. When she did call, she engaged him in an interminable discussion over what times were mutually convenient to each of them.

Her husband had asked her to consult a marriage counselor with him because he had been finding their life together bewildering and depressing. She had been alternately angry and critical, affectionate and giving, during the little over a year she and Philip had been married.

Alice had found the three years of their dating relationship pleasant and compatible at all levels; but once married, she could not cope with her feelings of being committed to and dependent on Philip. She established a rigid schedule for the responsibilities of their life together. "Everything in our marriage should be on a fifty-fifty basis," she outlined. "We will visit your family one week end a month, and mine one week end a month. . . ." Philip went along with her wishes. His first glimpse of the underlying problem came one night when they were making love. "I feel as if we are one person," he said softly. She replied: "Let's get something straight. I don't like that oneness business. We're two separate individuals. Besides, I think you've been getting too dependent on me."

He felt put off. The more he tried to clarify his idea that two people in love have a mutual need for each other that cannot be measured mathematically, the more she insisted that his dependency on her was abnormal. Hurt and angry, he began to strike back. Several times over the following months he screamed at her, "If you don't like the way things are going, pack your bags and get out." At other times, feeling more and more hopeless, he begged, "I need you, Alice. I want you. I don't understand why you always have to put down the idea of sharing."

Alice was afraid of sharing. Throughout a life of insecurity she had learned to count only on herself. When she was four, both her parents had been killed in an automobile crash. She and her two brothers were shifted about among several aunts and uncles. By the time she was sixteen she was an extremely self-contained and independent girl, admired by her friends and respected by her teachers not only for academic excellence, but also for working after school and in the summers to support herself. When she met Philip, she was working as a supervisor for the telephone company, where she made decisions easily and felt on top of her responsibilities.

As long as Alice remained aloof from any but the most superficial relationships with men she felt fine. She tended to date boys who were intellectually beneath her, and she always remained in command of the relationship. Only once before meeting her husband had she become involved with a man toward whom she felt a strong romantic and sexual attraction. Her ambivalence activated, she struggled back and forth between needing him and fearing his rejection, rebelling against the relationship and denying its significance. In the end, she abruptly stopped seeing him.

When she decided to marry, at thirty-one, it was not only because she felt that it was time for her to marry; she thought that she had found a man she could trust, who would respect her need for independence and, at the same time, give her the love and support she wanted. Unfortunately, she had underestimated the degree to which her need for independence clashed with any lasting commitment to a man. She had not considered how her inability to either lean on her husband to some degree or permit him to lean on her would produce a serious imbalance in their relationship and turn his otherwise normal dependency needs into a frantic and helpless bid for her love.

The majority of conflicts between married couples involve confusion over the meaning of dependency. This confusion is reinforced by traditional, though outmoded, assumptions that dependency is a sex-related characteristic. Women are supposed to be dependent. Men are denied the right to be dependent. Initiative and self-determination are unfeminine. Needing someone is unmasculine. Although the educational efforts of the women's liberation movement have done much to help change some misconceptions about femininity, there remains a deeply ingrained dogma that masculinity implies a kind of strength that precludes moments of helplessness.

As recently as ten years ago, it was common for women to arrive in a psychiatrist's office asking for help to keep their marriages and families together. The husband might have become cold and difficult. He might have found another woman he wanted to live with. His wife, feeling so dependent on the family structure whether she loved him or not, was terrified of what would happen to her if it collapsed. During the last six years a curious reversal has taken place. It is now common for the husband to be the one consulting the professional adviser with the hope of keeping his home intact, often "for the children's sake." The wife, on the other hand, is pressing for divorce, not necessarily because of an involvement with someone else but out of pent-up resentment combined with a determination to escape the "oppression" of her life and go out to "do her own thing."

"I haven't been in love with him for years," said one thirty-four-year-old woman who was contemplating divorce. "The only reason I haven't left before is because I was afraid he would fall apart. There's no one else. I would never marry again. Frankly, I'd just rather be on my own, work, take care of the children myself." Her husband commented: "I'd do anything to make it work. I haven't been able to sleep or concentrate on my work since she first started talking about wanting a divorce. I could find another woman, sure. But it's the children. I can't bear the thought of not living with the children. It's true, at work I have a lot of responsibilities. I handle them well. I don't lack initiative. But something has happened to me in our relationship at home. Over the years I've deferred more and more to her wishes. I thought I was pleasing her. As she has become more independent, I seem to have become more dependent."

In some cases, dependency needs are unusually strong to begin with. For such people, the closeness in marriage or in any love relationship forms a breeding ground for becoming so dependent that a loss of individuality can result. "I've lost interest in doing anything without my husband," said a twenty-three-year-old woman who had been married less than six months. "I used to play tennis, see a lot of my friends, go to films by myself. Before we got married I quit my job to stay home and take care of decorating the house. But now I don't want to do anything. I haven't called a girl friend in months. I'm tired all the time. I watch television during the day, but mostly I wait for Burt to come home. He likes to play golf on week ends. I hate that. I feel so lonely when he's not around." With him she felt alive and energetic. Without him she felt unmotivated, aimless. As long as she had been emotionally uninvolved with anyone, she was unaware of her potential for becoming so dependent.

The same kind of excessive dependency can be seen in work situations. Bill Follet had been conditioned by his upbringing to be very dependent, at first on the approval of his teachers, and later on the approval of his supervisors at work. He was a claims

manager for a large insurance company. His immediate supervisor was a vice-president of the company,
a volatile and demanding man who valued Bill's reliability but, at the same time, was frequently critical
of him. On several occasions he even blocked Bill's
transfer to a better position within the company so as
not to be bothered with finding a replacement. Bill's
moods fluctuated and were strongly influenced by his
boss's moods. Although he was indignant when he
learned that he had lost out on several promotions because of his boss's interference, he continued to work
at his job and still depended very much on the occasional word of praise he would glean from time to
time. He sometimes thought of leaving the company,
but never found the time or energy to look for another job. "I just don't seem to be able to let go of it,"
he observed. "It's as if I have no other choice."

Extreme dependency will cause a loss of self-
confidence and, with it, chronic depression. Dependency has a way of feeding on itself. The more Bill
Follet obtained the stingy recognition of his superiors,
the more his appetite for recognition increased.

People who have been hospitalized for long periods of time—whether for physical or emotional problems—lose the sense of competence with which they
previously dealt with life. Recent efforts to shorten
the hospital stay of patients with emotional disorders
have been based on the observation that long-term
hospitalization aggravates the sense of helplessness
originally activated by their fear and depression. After
months away from the demands of his ordinary life,
the individual may gradually become so adapted to a
less demanding routine that he loses confidence in his

ability to cope with everyday matters. Day-to-day life outside the hospital becomes unreal. He focuses more and more on the details of hospital living. The first visit out is often dreaded. "Can I make it? Will I fall apart? Do I really want to go out?" In spite of the deprivations that exist in institutional living, it is as if he must be weaned away from it in order to stand on his own again.

A similar treatment problem can be seen in caring for the aged. As long as they are in familiar surroundings, able to cope with the demands of daily life, elderly people can usually function well. An unexpected physical illness that forces them into a hospital or a nursing home often leads to a rapid deterioration in their ability to handle their own affairs. They become very dependent on the nurses for many things they had previously looked after themselves. If such a condition of enforced dependency continues for too long a time, many will find it impossible to ever return to a reasonable level of self-sufficiency.

The very points in life at which dependency needs are most likely to be a major source of conflict are points at which depression is likely to occur— adolescence, for example. The adolescent is engaged in a classic struggle between wanting independence from the family and wanting the security of knowing that the family is still there in case anything goes wrong. As Robert Frost wrote,

Home is the place where, when you have to go there,
They have to take you in . . .

Parents who fail to appreciate the delicate balance of needs within the teen-ager—how his overconfidence col-

lides with his fear of failure and his susceptibility to depression—can seriously compromise his growing sense of
self-reliance.

"All the time my dad communicates this lack of
confidence in me," said one sixteen-year-old boy. "He's
always putting me down. Compares me with guys who
are more athletic. Compares me with the brains in
school. Every time I make a mistake, even a small one,
like the time I took the wrong train to the country
and he had to wait an extra twenty minutes at the
station, he bawls me out. I depend on what he thinks
of me, more than I want to. He doesn't seem to realize
that."

Retirement is also a time for dependency and
depression. "I never realized how much I needed to
work. It's been difficult to get readjusted. After thirty
years with one company, going to the same office,
seeing the same friends, you get into a routine. Then,
all of a sudden, it's over. Pulled out from under you.
The children are gone. There's just my wife and me.
The one thing we can count on is getting older."

Extricating oneself from a dependent position is
bound to be painful. People can become as habituated
to a person or a job as they can to a drug. The withdrawal symptoms can be just as severe.

Complicating the picture is the fact that helplessness can itself be a position of strength. A considerable
amount of unhealthy gain can be derived from being
dependent. When being helpless becomes its own reward and the dependent person realizes the full reaches
of his influence, he can dominate a situation simply by
doing nothing at all. Any group—particularly a family

—can be immobilized by this maneuver. "My mother-in-law has us all in a bind," said one man. "She won't drive a car—says she can't. She doesn't help my wife with the housework—says she doesn't feel strong enough to. She won't do anything to find an apartment of her own—says that she couldn't bear the loneliness of living by herself. She's been in our home for six years. She's only fifty-seven. She came to live with us when my father-in-law died. Every time we make a move to get her out, she gets conveniently sick. It never proves to be anything serious, just enough to keep us from doing anything. She runs our home, without lifting a finger."

The person who uses helplessness to control usually requires a collaborator, someone who encourages his dependency and derives some gratification from it—or who at least does not appreciate the nature of the interdependent system. Any effort to restore a healthy sense of independence in such a person will involve a change in the attitudes of those who, unwittingly or in the service of their own needs, may have been encouraging the persistence of his helplessness.

13

Depressogenic Environments

THERE IS A CONSTANT INTERACTION between every human being and his environment. This interaction is always in a state of flux. When something happens in a person's environment, he reacts to it. This, in turn, produces a response from the environment to which he will again respond.

Considerable variation exists with regard to what degree people are susceptible to external influences. Some are highly sensitive to what goes on around them; others are not. For those who are, the environment can have a profound effect on mood. Their world may regularly confirm a healthy sense of self-esteem, allow for the expression of feelings, and provide them with an atmosphere of hope. On the other hand, if their environment provides no ego support, prevents them from becoming self-reliant, repeatedly stirs up hostility and at the same time blocks its release, provokes unnecessary guilt, or causes them to feel lonely and rejected, it can be called depressogenic. Such an environment will provoke moods of depression in the majority of people who inhabit it.

Consider, in its simplest terms, the impact of a sarcastic remark. It is essentially a put-down. To what extent will it hurt the person toward whom it is directed? It depends on how much he relies for self-esteem on the opinion of the person who made the remark and how repeatedly he is exposed to such attacks.

Consider the following dialogue:

HUSBAND: I'll be about an hour late for dinner tonight. I have to meet Bob for drinks to talk about my life insurance policy.

WIFE: Go ahead. Have a good time without me. It doesn't matter what time you come home.

HUSBAND (*feeling slightly wounded and agitated*): It does matter. But this is the only time we can get together. It's important. We're not going to have a ball. We're going over things that have to do with our financial security—yours as well as mine. (Thinking to himself, What have I done wrong now?)

The provocation here is the husband's announcement that he will be late for dinner. His wife's reaction is sarcastic. It is designed to hurt, to make him feel guilty. It succeeds because he loves her and is concerned about her feelings and how she regards him. If he has had a long-standing problem in apportioning his time, her reaction may well be warranted. On the other hand, if she is hypersensitive to being rejected, or competitive and essentially envious of his opportunity to spend an hour with a friend and business associate, her response is skewed; that is, based more on her own needs than on the reality of the situation. In that event she is contributing to a depressogenic climate in her home.

A depressogenic environment fails to provide the individual with adequate support for his self-esteem—often, in fact, actively undermining it—or repeatedly activates emotions and conflicts that the susceptible individual cannot handle without becoming depressed. The effect of such an environment may be mild or severe, depending on the intensity and persistence of the depressogenic factors.

Unless an individual is already depressed, it is usually possible for him to overlook or respond with brief anger to provocations from people who matter little to him. But if he is attacked by someone whose love and respect are highly valued, the feelings of hurt, guilt, or helplessness that result can have a considerable impact on him. This is especially true when criticism does not focus on the subject under discussion, but consists instead of irrelevant and denigrating comments about the kind of person he is. When a parent corrects a child by saying: "Stop that! You're going to break it!" the effect on the child is quite different from that produced by an exclamation such as "Stop that! How can you be so *dumb!*" As transactional analysts such as Eric Berne and James Harris have described, adults frequently interact with each other—verbally and nonverbally—in ways reminiscent of parent-child relationships, going after egos instead of issues.

Every human being depends to some degree on the way those he trusts see him. His idea of the kind of person he is can either be clarified or confused through their opinions. A compliment from a superior at work confirms his own idea that he has been doing a good job. Being passed over for a deserved promotion, or being promptly criticized when he makes a mistake and barely recognized when he performs well, will generate in most people a mixture of hurt, resentment, and doubt about their own abilities, and can lead to depression. To be on the receiving end of an "I'm O.K., you're not O.K." interaction in a marriage will shatter anyone's sense of self-worth, unless he is so insulated and unresponsive that the critical and depreciatory communications fail to reach him.

If the evaluations delivered to a person from those close to him are confused and distorted, they will predictably have a detrimental effect on his self-image. Questions thrown out more as accusations—"Why are you always so angry?" "Why are you so selfish and unappreciative?" "Why aren't you a better wife?" —will produce an inner state of confusion and doubt in the person to whom they are directed. Even when there is a grain of truth in them, they are more likely to provoke defensiveness than insight. When they are untrue and unsubstantiated and more reflective of the inner conflicts and distorted perceptions of the one who is criticizing than of the behavior of the one being criticized, they can seriously threaten his sense of identity.

A depressogenic environment is made up of thousands of verbal and nonverbal exchanges that take place daily and that stir up in the vulnerable individual a loss of self-esteem, guilt, inexpressible anger, a chronic sense of not being understood. The following conversation between a father and his son illustrates the process of inducing guilt:

> FATHER: Why couldn't you come by to see us last week end?
>
> SON: Mary and I had to take the children to a picnic. I thought I told you about it.
>
> FATHER: I don't recall. You don't seem to spend as much time with your mother and me as you did.
>
> SON (*slightly annoyed*): We're here today. Besides, we spent a week with you last month, most of my vacation.
>
> FATHER: Somehow I feel you're a stranger. I'm not getting any younger. Your mother gets very upset when you can't come.

If his son had been really avoiding him, the father in this example would probably have had a just cause to be critical. As it happens, his son, daughter-in-law, and grandchildren had been spending one or two week ends each month with him. What he basically resented was the complete economic and personal independence his children had attained. He needed the control he had once held over his family, and now most of it was gone. He himself was depressed, but because he would not acknowledge it his reaction took the form of making them feel guilty, as if they had rejected him. This did not detract from his loneliness and his genuine wish to see them, but it did provoke a sense of guilt in them and create a depressogenic atmosphere in his home.

Within a family or an organization, an environment which is depressogenic for one person may not be for another. A young lawyer was repeatedly frustrated and depressed as long as he worked for a large and tightly organized firm. He had no clients under his direct supervision. All his work was meticulously checked. He was anxious for greater responsibility, but knew it would be years away.

He had been an outstanding student in college and had not required the reassurance of grades to bolster his self-esteem. He was also a "self-starter," and found it difficult to operate within the rigid lines of the law firm. After a period of discouragement punctuated by heated arguments with his immediate supervisor, he quit and found another position in a smaller and less prestigious firm, where the lines of command were not so stringently drawn and he had immediate access to any senior member. He was encouraged to take on as much responsibility as he could handle, and he approached his work with renewed hope and enthusiasm.

Even as a rigidly structured organization may be depressogenic for a self-actualizing individual, a more loosely organized group may be depressogenic for someone who requires a high degree of order to feel secure and function most effectively: "I just couldn't get my bearings in the last job I had. I was never sure what was expected of me. There wasn't much feedback and I was left pretty much on my own." Two years after graduation, this young scientist had obtained a good position with a well-known company in which every individual was given a good deal of freedom and responsibility. He was extremely dependent on the opinions of others. When left to his own devices, he would work ten and twelve hours a day, perfectionistically, never knowing how to set limits on his efforts. In his job he became increasingly unsure of himself and afraid that he would be fired for doing incompetent work.

Finally he decided that it would be better for him to find a more structured situation. He obtained a job teaching at a graduate school, where, being better able to define his responsibilities and his place within the organization, he felt quite comfortable and did extremely well in his work.

Some environments, however, are basically depressogenic to practically everyone who works within them. If, for example, the texture of an organization becomes too complex and constricted, as within many bureaucracies, the net effect can be stifling both for those who work in the organization and for those who have to deal with it.

Individual judgment gives way to forms and procedures. As the workers adapt more and more successfully to the system, they lose their decision-making abilities and flexibility vanishes. Constructive action is replaced by compulsiveness, by a series of delays and Kafka-like levels through which each and every item must pass, whether it takes weeks, months, or years.

The lack of responsiveness within such an environment has such a subtly depressing quality that it can conceal from those within it their own inner sense of depression. "I didn't know I was depressed all those years—not until I retired," said one company employee. "Everyone else seemed to be in the same boat. I thought it was just the normal way to be."

One of the characteristics of certain depressogenic environments is that they are composed largely of people who themselves are caught up in states of chronic depression, often without realizing it, and often as a result of conflicts that originate in their personal lives and are carried over into work. Frequently the more energetic and independent people leave. Those who remain exude an air of futility that seems appropriate to the setting, and continually reinforce each other's depression.

For depression is contagious. Nurses and doctors who work with depressed patients in psychiatric hospitals often leave at the end of the day exhausted and feeling pointless. Surrounded for hours by patients who complain about their unhappiness, who resist efforts to reassure and encourage them, and who stub-

bornly refuse to socialize with others or attend recre-
ational activities, the staff members often find themselves taking on the pessimism and hopelessness to
which they are exposed. This can occur even though
they are professionally trained and realize that the ultimate prognosis for many of these patients is excellent.

The depressed person, in other words, helps create his own depressogenic environment. "I love Karl. I
really do. But unless you can do something to help him,
doctor, I don't know how much more I can take." A
forty-three-year-old woman was describing what it
was like to live with her depressed husband, the effect
it had been having on her. "I'm normally a cheerful
person. I think that a solution can be found to almost
any problem. But during the last year Karl has been so
pessimistic and moody that I'm beginning to get that
way myself. We can't ever make plans. It's as if there
isn't any future. He drains me."

Within any group—a family, a business, a government—the most important figures influencing the psychological quality of the environment are those at the
top. In business it is the chief executive officer and his
immediate associates. In a religious order it is the superior. In the home it is the parent, or parents, who
exert the strongest influence in setting the tone of the
environment. Every group takes its character to a significant degree from its leadership. If the leadership is
depressogenic, the environment will be too.

Harold Strange was appointed chief executive officer of a major chemical company at the age of forty-
seven. Although he had little administrative experience,
he was asked to run an organization with thousands of
employees.

Strange, unaware of his lack of executive aptitude, thought of himself as a good leader and rejected the suggestion that he might spend a few months at an advanced management training program. He was by nature an extremely distrustful and sensitive person—sensitive to his own feelings, but not to those of others. Slow in making decisions, he liked to think about issues for a long time before committing himself. He was often unaware of, and unresponsive to, the needs of those beneath him.

He preferred to keep a firm control over everything that happened in the company. He did not want any individual to become so prominent or so powerful that he might jeopardize his command. Although slow to respond to ordinary suggestions or requests, and offering little or no support to the more energetic or creative members of his group, he was still extremely vulnerable to being forced to comply with demands made by senior executives in positions of strength. If, for example, the vice-president in charge of sales, with a long history of excellent customer relationships, demanded a larger staff and budget and offered his resignation as an alternative if his request was denied, Harold Strange would grant it, however reluctantly. By contrast, if an innovative plan to develop new business leads was presented to him in an open and constructive way, he would sit on it for weeks and sometimes months. If he finally gave the go-ahead, he would fail to back the strategy at key moments.

His tendency to withdraw, except when he was bludgeoned into action, caused a serious vacuum in leadership. This was further aggravated by his need to divide and conquer. He played one lieutenant against another, the research and development group against the sales executives, the board of directors against his own hand-selected staff. His purpose: to maintain control. The result: a seriously depressogenic environment.

When Harold Strange arrived at the company, there were half a dozen bright and energetic leaders in various positions within it. One of them, anticipating trouble, quit as soon as he learned who was taking over. During the next three years there was a gradual attrition; one after another, key members of the company resigned to find other places where they could work effectively.

One executive in particular experienced a serious depression before he could bring himself to relocate. Although skeptical, Ed Fosse had been willing to give the new chief executive officer a chance. Six months after Harold Strange's arrival, Fosse presented him with an important blueprint for rehauling the marketing approach for one of their most important products. Strange sat on the plan for three months and, when questioned, would reply, "I'll get to it as soon as I can." Subsequently, Fosse began to receive increasingly confused and mixed messages from Strange's office. First he was told his budget for the coming year would be reduced because of smaller profit margins. Then he was sent a note commending him on a report he had given before a meeting of the board.

At a small conference of executives he made a mildly critical remark indicating his annoyance at the delay in hearing from Strange about his marketing plan. Three weeks later he was called into Strange's office, where he was confronted with his remark. "Ed, I understand that you're seriously critical of the way I run this outfit," said his boss. "If you don't like it here, you can certainly leave. Your work is, frankly, not that impressive anyway."

One month later, Fosse received a commentary on his plan. Strange remarked that it was good, but added that the timing for such an approach was poor. Fosse's response to this event was frustration and self-doubt. Losing perspective into his initial evaluation of Strange, he began to feel that he was losing his own touch, that perhaps his work had indeed fallen off. He became worried and agitated, found it hard to sleep at night, and at moments felt as if his career were coming to an end. He had worked for this company for over ten years, and until now had never considered going elsewhere.

The causal factors for his depressive response were evident. A sensitive person, he required some recognition for his work from those in authority. Had Strange come right out and told him that he wasn't going to support his work, he could have handled this overt rejection firmly and definitively. But Strange didn't do that. Instead, what he communicated added up to such ambivalent messages as: "We want to keep you here, but we're not going to give you any support"; and "I'm not interested in your gripes and criticisms, but if you exert enough pressure—threaten and berate me—I might just give in to your requests."

Finally, there was Strange's pathological need to maintain control at all times, even at the expense of the company's growth. To ensure such control, he instinctively demoralized his subordinates. Four years later, after a disastrous profit-loss statement, the board of directors asked for Strange's resignation. By then the key positions in the firm were occupied only by executives who could cope with, and at times flourish within, the depressogenic nature of the environment he had created.

The principles involved in the creation of a depressogenic environment are similar whether an organization is large or small, such as a family. The most commonly employed tactics used to induce depression within families include:

Keeping an individual from finding some degree of independence, while one or several members of the family maintain control

Stirring up separation anxiety; that is, encouraging a dependency that convinces the more dependent member that he cannot possibly survive without their emotional support

Delivering ambivalent messages that undermine self-esteem and at the same time block legitimate self-defense, such as "I love you, in spite of the kind of person you are"

Repeatedly provoking guilt by making the other person feel responsible, regardless of the facts

Misinterpreting intentions and motives so that the more insecure member begins to doubt his own perceptions, even though they are more accurate

Contaminating family interactions with a competitiveness that stems from envy and jealousy

Providing a monotonous, unstimulating environment that resists any effort to introduce humor, spontaneity, and joy

Refusing to permit any open show of emotion, and in particular healthy reactions of anger

Using a chronic state of depression to express anger indirectly, making others feel helpless, guilty, and confused in the process

Blocking open and direct communication

During the last ten years therapists have become more aware of the importance of dealing with the entire family and not limiting therapy to the person who is declared the "patient." In the earlier psychoanalytic approach to therapy there was an assumption that once the depressed individual recovered he would be able to cope with any but the most destructive environmental conditions. It became obvious, however, that many patients would reach a plateau of improvement from which they could not move on. This was at first interpreted as "resistance." But now it is clear that frequently members of the patient's family may have a vested interest in keeping him from pulling out of his depression. In such cases, therapists often attempt to involve the families in the therapeutic experience in order to modify depressogenic elements in the home. Sometimes the patient, with new insights, can succeed in altering the attitudes of other family members by himself. Sometimes such a complete break-down in communication within the family takes place that the patient has no choice but to remove himself from it.

In their book *The Intimate Enemy*, psychiatrist George Bach and Peter Wyden, describing various de-structive ways of channeling hostility between mar-ried partners, have called attention to a particular sadistic ploy that they term "gaslighting." Gaslighting, which involves chipping away at the victim's percep-tion of himself and of his surroundings, is a term derived from the film *Gaslight*, in which Ingrid Berg-man played a young bride being driven out of her mind by her husband. Among other fiendish maneu-vers, Charles Boyer, as her husband, kept turning the lights up and down, but denied that they were chang-ing. His wife was torn between accepting her own perception of the fact that the lights were flickering and his insistence that they were not. Although Boyer's intentions—thwarted, fortunately, by the arrival of Joseph Cotten—were more sinister, variations on this theme seen in everyday life generally lead to depression in the victims.

In the following example, an adolescent girl's de-pression could be accounted for by the use of modified gaslighting techniques on the part of her mother. "I haven't any confidence in myself," she said. "I don't feel attractive. I'm all right as a student, but nothing special. I don't know what I want to do with my life. I don't mind that—I'm only seventeen. What really gets to me is that I can't think about myself in a con-structive way. I'm too busy thinking about the way in which my mother looks at me.

"She calls me fat and stupid. And then, when I cry, she asks me what I'm upset about. I got angry at her a few times. She acted really hurt, as if I had done something awful. She accused me of being ungrateful for all she had done for me.

"Done for me? What? I wanted to go away to college. We could afford it. I could get some state aid. She was against it. When I came home late a few times from a dance, she called me a whore and a slut. It makes you not care any more. I can't please her. I can't please myself.

"I don't get any support from my dad. He's quiet, and he never speaks up for himself. Mom told me that she would have left him a year or two after they were married, but she couldn't for my sake. Whenever I try to talk with him about anything serious, he pushes me away. I feel awful about him. He seems like such a tragic figure. I can't understand why he stayed with her. She treats him as if he were nothing, less than nothing."

Rigid, self-centered, guilt-inducing, domineering, this girl's mother was the key influence in the character of the family. She had succeeded, over a period of years, in encouraging her husband to withdraw into his own private world, while repeatedly demoralizing her daughter. Her unconscious motives: competition, to express her envy of her daughter's youthfulness and attractiveness; control, to keep her daughter from becoming independent of her; denial, to focus attention on the problems and difficulties of other family members and keep criticism away from herself. Her husband had long since entered a chronic depression. Her daughter, acutely depressed in her attempt to break away from her mother's influence, had sought counseling to help her in her efforts toward independence.

B. F. Skinner has pointed out that "gamblers appear to violate the law of effect because they continue to play even though their net reward is negative." In other words, the player wins often enough so that even though he loses frequently, and—because the odds are stacked against him—will lose in the end, he keeps on playing. Skinner attributes this phenomenon to the influence of what he calls a variable-ratio schedule of reinforcement. A similar process can be seen in human relationships. "I love you" can be communicated in word and action just often enough to keep the other person caught in the relationship, even though he is repeatedly subjected to indifference and at times contempt and will, like the gambler, lose in the end. In the game of dating, one of the most effective ways to force the more involved person to be "hung up" is to activate his anxiety by the conditioning effect of such on-again, off-again messages.

One young woman described her dating experience as follows: "I can't get him out of my mind. One week end he takes me to Nassau and tells me I'm his life. The next week he disappears completely for ten days, and when he comes back he acts as though I'm just another date. He even tells me about other girls he takes out. But whenever I build up the energy to break it off, he comes on strong again, telling me that someday, somehow, we'll live together. Sometimes I just want to die. I can't think of any other way to get rid of him."

The fact that a situation or an environment is depressogenic may not become apparent until it changes in some significant way. When changes are extensive —when a tightly structured environment begins to come apart—the conflict between the old way of doing things and the new produces confusion. The more strongly conditioned an individual has been to the previous structure, the more likely he is to experience depression in trying to adapt to the new one.

Bryan Donnelly was a priest. He was forty-one when he was transferred by his order to teach in a small college in Kansas. He hated his assignment. He had received his Ph.D. in physics at Harvard the previous year and had wanted to pursue his research, but he had not been permitted to do so.

On becoming a priest over a decade earlier, he had taken his vows of poverty and obedience and had willingly given up the option of having a family and children to pursue a religious life. A good student, he had selected his particular order because of its emphasis on intellectual achievement. Obedient and used to taking orders, he had accommodated well to the highly rigid and structured seminary life, only occasionally becoming annoyed—but keeping it to himself—when he felt that petty considerations dominated common sense. After ten years, he had lost the ability to select his own goals and make decisions for himself.

Following the brief reign of Pope John XXIII, the Roman Catholic Church began to experience major and minor upheavals. One of the basic changes that occurred was a modification in the role of authority. Members within religious orders pressed for the right to have more of a voice in selecting the direction of their lives. Authority became less openly arbitrary. Religious dress became optional. Seminarians no longer had to live in isolated, faraway institutions, but might find their own apartments in large cities and attend classes at theological centers of various sects.

At this point the incidence of depression among clergymen began to mount. Why? In the first place, some priests had been chronically depressed to begin with. It was only when the structure changed and required a greater degree of individual initiative that such a depressed group could be identified. Secondly, although authority was now less rigid and participation was being encouraged, this shift required a major change in the thinking of superiors who had once held absolute sway over subordinates. "This is your assignment" was replaced by "Will you consider accepting this assignment?" Nonverbally, however, behind the question lay either the original order itself—comply! —or a major withdrawal from authority, with an implicit rejection: "Find your own way, but without direction or support from us. We will not rule where we are not wanted." This mixed message provoked depression among many priests, including Bryan Donnelly.

At the same time, the public prestige of the clergy of all religions was waning. The self-esteem that for centuries had been attached to being a priest, minister, or rabbi was no longer being reinforced by an attitude of awe and respect from the laity. Behind this was an even deeper problem: a crisis in faith.

A crisis in authority, a crisis in faith, and a loss of prestige in the community jolted the average clergyman, especially those over forty. It jolted Bryan Donnelly. He became depressed, and began to seriously consider giving up the religious life to find a new life for himself outside.

When any organization undergoes a major change —even when there is hope of restructuring it on a new and more effective level—some of its members who have been chronically depressed may become aware of it for the first time, whereas others may become depressed in response to the change itself. For either group of people, such a disruption offers each individual a real opportunity to resolve his own emotional conflicts and learn from depression, and also to work together with others to build environments that will not be depressogenic.

14

Living
with
Someone
Who
Is
Depressed

DIANA BRENT wondered why she had not heard a thing from her close friend Laurie in nearly two months. At first she assumed that Laurie was too busy to return her calls. As the weeks passed she began to wonder whether she might have done something to offend her, but could not come up with anything in particular. A feeling of hurt gradually gave way to annoyance: "At least she could call me." Finally, feeling quite rejected, she came to the conclusion that she had simply lost a good friend for no apparent reason.

What Diana did not know, because Laurie failed to tell her, was that Laurie was depressed. Being depressed, she had withdrawn from her friends, not wanting to see anyone, not wanting to impose her mood and unhappiness on them. She also did not want them to engage in a futile and irritating attempt to "cheer her up."

Because withdrawal—not wanting to be with people and not wanting to communicate with them when they are around—is a common sign of being depressed, the "other person" frequently feels that the depressed individual is pushing him away. "My wife just isn't the same," commented one man. "When I try to talk to her about business, or friends, or redecorating the house, I not only get no enthusiasm, I sometimes don't get any response at all, or at best a monosyllabic one. For weeks now she's shown no affection toward me. When I bring it up, she just apologizes and says that she'll try to do better. When I ask her what's wrong, I get nowhere. And when I ask her whether I've done anything to upset her, she says no, but she acts as if I have. The net result of all this is that I'm getting pulled down. I feel terribly responsible, but I don't know what for."

The first assumption many a person makes when living with, or relating to, a depressed person is that somehow he is responsible for the other's unhappiness. The guilt that accompanies this assumption often makes the individual want to avoid the depressed person. Feeling guilty, especially when it is difficult to understand why, makes such an individual feel uneasy and irritable with the depressed person who stirs it up. One therapist, when asked whether working with depressed patients made him uncomfortable or impatient, replied, "Less than it might, because I can have more perspective than the person's family; I *know* I haven't been the cause of his unhappiness."

The likelihood of feeling rejected or guilty is greater when there seems to be no reason for the depressed person to be depressed. When there is a well-defined and easily recognized cause for the unhappiness, neither the unhappy person nor those around him need to puzzle over what is happening. But when depression follows a presumably happy event—the birth of a child or a significant promotion at work or a move to a new home—the apparent lack of connection between the two is confusing, leaving everyone to wonder who and what are responsible.

It is not unusual for the individual who has never been depressed to underestimate both the pain the depressed person experiences and the length of time the depression may last. "Pull yourself together, Helen; your mother's been dead for over three months"; and "How can you say our marriage is terrible when we've had eight really great years?"; and "I just don't understand how you can be so discouraged about your appearance that you don't want to go anywhere." Comments such as these, expressed in a perplexed and angry way, are common responses to the depressed person when those near him lack any insight into the nature and causes of the mood.

People who have never experienced depression tend to be impatient with the depressed person. It is an impatience caused partly by the slowness and indecisiveness that go along with being depressed and the persistence with which depression hangs on. It is an impatience that is a response to the underlying anger and hostility often lurking behind the depression.

When someone is anxious, it is likely to stir up the

anxiety of those around him. When someone is depressed, it is likely to have a depressive effect on those around him. Therefore, those who would like to be helpful to the depressed person frequently find themselves unable to be empathetic because of the feeling of futility they may have when in contact with him. Of course, this only serves to reinforce the depressed individual's feeling of hopelessness and his conviction that he is rejected and misunderstood.

It is especially difficult for advocates of the supremacy of will power to understand or cope with someone who is depressed. Such a person mistakenly assumes that "you are what you choose to be" and sees a deliberateness in the depressed person's attitudes and behavior that he finds intolerable and provocative. Psychiatrist Lawrence Kubie once defined will power as the energy required to overcome a neurotic block such as a phobic or compulsive fear. For the depressed individual, will power implies the energy required just to go on with daily life, attending to various tasks, seeing people, communicating, in spite of the underlying urge to withdraw. But for those who have never been depressed and who honestly believe that both mood and self-esteem are a matter of forcing oneself to feel cheerful, depression seems a most mysterious and contrary process indeed.

One mildly depressed woman was having difficulty falling asleep at night and would wake up an hour or so early in the morning. During the day she was tired. "It's your own fault that you're tired during the day," reasoned her husband. "You have to *make* yourself go to bed earlier and lie there until you get to sleep. I get angry with you because you're just not trying." The more he admonished her to correct her sleep difficulty, the more trouble she had getting to sleep at all, and bedtime became for her a time to be dreaded.

How one reacts to the depressed individual obviously depends on the form the depression takes and the response of the depressed person to his mood. It is frustrating when someone will not or cannot take steps to help himself. "My daughter is having awful problems in her marriage," said one elderly woman. "Her husband has found someone else. She knows about it. But neither of them wants a divorce. My daughter is miserable. She cries all the time. I want to help her, but she won't let me. I suggested she talk with a psychiatrist. She said no, she didn't need to. Besides, she's afraid he might tell her to pack her bags and leave. She doesn't want to do that. I can't tell you how upset and helpless I feel." This woman, having had episodes of depression at various times during her life, was not angry or impatient with her daughter. What she did feel was frustration: "I know she needs professional help, and basically she does too, but she just won't do anything about it."

The most difficult type of depression to be in contact with is not the most dramatic, but the most indirect. It is when the person himself does not recognize his depression, or seeks to solve his conflicts through behavior such as the excessive use of alcohol, or falls back on blaming everything and everyone for his misery and unhappiness, that those around him will find it hard to empathize and difficult to help. By contrast, when the depression is experienced clearly and directly, and when the depressed person can understand to some degree why he is down, it is much easier to reach out to him. Rollo May, in his book *Paulus*, wrote about the depressive episodes that Paul Tillich experienced: "His depressions never made the rest of us depressed because they were open. . . . If we admit our depression openly and freely, those around us get from it an experience of freedom rather than the depression itself."

The more intense kinds of depressive reactions can be frightening. "My husband slept only two or three hours a night," said a thirty-four-year-old woman. "In spite of this he went to work and put in a full day. By the time he came home, he was wiped out. He often went into the bedroom, closed the door, and cried. I could hear him. If I went in to talk to him, he would accept my comfort for a while, but sooner or later he would get up from the bed and pace around restlessly. He wouldn't watch television or read. He never talked about suicide, but he seemed so upset I was terrified that he might do something to himself. He said he wouldn't. He said such ideas had never entered his mind. But I just couldn't understand why he was so upset.

"I've been down, but I usually know why, and it rarely lasts more than a day or so. With him, it kept going on for weeks. I couldn't stop being afraid until, with therapy, he started to show some improvement. And even now, six months later, if he gets up during the night or seems a little preoccupied, I become frightened. I have to learn to trust all over again."

One's reaction to the depressed person is strongly influenced by some of the specific conflicts that are caused by, or contribute to, the depression. Dependency, for example. "Almost from the beginning of our marriage, Neil wanted to be with me all the time when he wasn't at work," commented his wife. "At first it was romantic. But now, two years later, it's stifling. He used to have a lot of interests. He used to seem independent and decisive—the kind of man I wanted. But now it's like having a second child around the house. I have to make whatever plans there are. He spends hours in front of the television set. I get the distinct feeling that he needs me in an unhealthy way —that if anything happened to me he'd fall apart. It's an awful responsibility. It literally turns me off. I love him and I need him, but not this way."

A loss of sexual desire is another example. It is not unusual for a depressed man, whatever his age, to lose sexual interest and potency. This can easily be misinterpreted by his wife or by anyone else with whom he has been sexually intimate as a sexual rejection. "My husband hasn't made love to me in months. We used to have a good sexual relationship. Now I wonder if he's found someone else. For a while I kept pushing him about it, and then the more we tried, the less he could do. I wish I knew what was wrong."

How one reacts to the depressed person is also influenced by one's own personality. It is easier to understand what the depressed person is going through if one has experienced some measure of depression oneself. The person who is afraid of his own emotions will be especially stirred up by another's depression.

The husband of one depressed woman was so frightened of feeling depressed himself that he found it necessary to separate from his wife until she started therapy. "Being around her scared me, I don't know why. I couldn't say or do anything to comfort her. I was tongue-tied. I finally had to leave for a while. I was only making her worse by losing my temper. She realized it had nothing to do with my love for her. I just couldn't handle it."

Each person's sensitivity to taking the blame on himself varies, and those who are most inclined to feel "it's my fault" will also be the most likely to assume the responsibility for the depressed person's unhappiness. The difficulty a person has in accepting criticism and anger will also affect his attitude. As the depressed person recovers, he will be freer to express his anger appropriately and to be more aggressive. If those living with him find it hard to cope with this change because of their own difficulty in handling anger, three things can happen: first, they may try to get the person to suppress his emotions again; second, they may enter into open conflict with him; third, they may become depressed themselves.

The father of one sixteen-year-old boy described how, as his son pulled out of a depression, there were outbursts of anger which the family found hard to handle: "Bill was always a good boy . . . did well in school . . . was fun to have around. He never gave us any grief. Then, when he was fifteen, he became sullen and morose. Something was bothering him, but he wouldn't tell us what. His work fell off in school, and he began skipping classes. He wouldn't see any of his friends. On the advice of our family doctor we took him for some counseling. After a few weeks he began to have outbursts of anger at his mother and me. We weren't used to it. He accused us of interfering with his independence, of keeping him from growing up. At other times he would just be mad because something went wrong—dinner was later than he expected or a trip that he planned had to be canceled.

"It was like having a stranger in the house. Worse yet, it was painful because we didn't know what to do. What he said hurt our feelings, especially mine. Also, I was brought up not to express any disrespect toward my parents, and sometimes I came down hard on him. Now I can see that he had to go through that phase. Getting out the anger was part of breaking away from us and getting out of his depression."

Changing the way in which close relatives, friends, and co-workers relate to the depressed person is part of helping him recover from his depression with insight. There are certain important principles involved:

Understand that the depressed person really hurts. Regardless of whether the circumstances seem to justify the extent of his reaction, his distress is real and not feigned. Depression has been called a tactic to manipulate and control others. It is not. While it is true that people who tend to be manipulative may use depression for that purpose, depression, in and of itself, is not a ploy unless the personality of the depressed individual is already constructed that way. Even when the depression expresses anger or is used as a plea for understanding, it still hurts. Any effort to suggest that the mood of the depressed person is false will clearly reinforce his sense of being alienated and rejected.

Empathize, rather than sympathize, with the depressed person. To feel sorry for him only reinforces his feeling of hopelessness and confirms his lowered sense of self-esteem. It may also make him feel more helpless and dependent.

Don't confront the depressed person with unbearable truths. A forty-two-year-old man decided to clear the air in his marriage by admitting to his wife that he had been having an affair. His wife had been somewhat depressed for several months, following her father's death. Not heeding her mood, he relieved his own guilt by his confession—a highly dubious tactic under any circumstance—and thereby triggered a suicide attempt. When controversial issues are to be discussed effectively, it is usually best to wait until the individual is no longer depressed.

Provide hope realistically. Offering reassurance to the depressed person—telling him that everything will be all right—is important, but must be done judiciously. He does not feel, at that moment, that everything will be all right. Even though he needs encouragement, he is not likely to trust it. Moreover, if any real dangers exist—financial difficulties, the threat of divorce, a child's illness—he does not want them denied. Pretending that there is nothing wrong when something is very wrong is hardly the way to offer reassurance. One woman, to help her depressed husband feel better, found herself telling him that she loved him and "would stay with him forever," even though she had been regularly consulting a counselor for months to help her cope with what she considered to be a basically poor marriage. The reassurance did not work because, in spite of it, he was picking up all kinds of nonverbal messages from her that contradicted what she said.

Any reassurance offered should be based on fact. The depressed person—whether in that mood for a day, a week, or a month—has lost perspective. When he is depressed he feels as if things have always been the way they are, even though he knows it isn't true.

A man who had been a fine father, a good husband, and a successful businessman felt, while he was depressed, that he had failed on all three counts. His wife, seeing that he had no appreciation of himself as he really was, found ways and means to gently remind him of how much he meant to her and the children. Intuitively, she did so quietly, repeatedly, without overdoing it, often by dropping a reassuring remark here and there that he heard even though he did not immediately respond to it. Therapists know that the tenacity of depression often works against reassurance, and that too great an emphasis on the positive aspects of the individual's personality and life will only drive him further into depression, as if he must prove to himself that things are hopeless and that he is without worth.

The extent to which one becomes involved in trying to help the depressed person depends upon the nature of their relationship. Obviously, it would be imprudent for a casual friend to take a major responsibility for helping someone cope with depression. He can make it clear that he is available. He can be supportive. But he should not push beyond the limits set by the nature of the relationship itself.

For a close friend or relative, however, the responsibility is greater. "It isn't just that I want to do something for him—I have to," said the wife of a man who had been experiencing depressive moods for nearly three years. Finally, on the advice of a friend, she consulted a psychiatrist. "I feel foolish being here," she remarked. "I don't really know what you can do to help."

The psychiatrist was able to outline for her a strategy to persuade her husband to start treatment. He was also able to help her reshape her thinking about her husband's depression. "I had begun to think he didn't care about me any more. I couldn't help regarding his anxiety as a kind of weakness. I thought our marriage was falling apart. Now I can see that all these things were the result and not the root cause of his depression. You've given me hope."

The family of the depressed person plays a vital role in hastening his recovery. By understanding the nature of depression and offering him the support he needs, they can help him work through his depression and together they can evolve a sounder system of relationships.

15

The
Anatomy
of
Melancholia

EVEN THOUGH THE MAJORITY of people who experience depression do not become severely depressed, some do. There are times when depression is clearly a medical problem and warrants sound professional care. The manic-depressive reaction, the agitated depression, the paranoid form of depression, the state of severe panic that can overwhelm the depressed person—each of these conditions calls for rather specific psychotherapeutic and biological approaches to treatment, sometimes including hospitalization.

There has been a debatable move within psychiatry to dismiss traditional diagnostic thinking and replace it with concepts that envision the depressed person as a part of an interactional system encompassing other people in his environment. This attitude, which leads to a refusal to define the patient as "sick," has much to say in its favor. Diagnosis can easily become a form of labeling that can be misleading and compromising. Because of the forbidding quality of the term "mental illness" implicit in diagnostic concepts, many people who are depressed are afraid to acknowledge it and hence do not take steps to get help when they need it.

The traditional approach whereby the patient is singled out as being "sick" can lead to underestimating the extent to which he is indeed a victim of others who may require his incapacitation in order to preserve their own equilibrium; his recovery may force a major reshuffling in personal relationships. Moreover, the labels themselves have an unfair impact on the outlook for improvement. Terms like "schizo-affective disorder" and "manic-depressive psychosis" convey an unwarranted impression of incurability, even though many patients with these diagnoses have excellent chances of recovery, especially since the advent of such biological treatments as phenothiazines and lithium. There is also a strong cultural bias to diagnosis. In England, for instance, the diagnosis of manic-depressive reaction is frequently used for patients who in the United States would be diagnosed as schizophrenic.

Diagnostic concepts can also be misleading when they are misinterpreted to imply that people who do not fit into specific categories of emotional disorders —who do not manifest hallucinations, delusions, or serious changes in mood—are necessarily whole and intact. Nothing could be further from the truth. Wilhelm Reich, who defined personality types such as the compulsive, the hysterical, and the narcissistic, was among the first to point out the fact that character structure can be as much of a problem for the individual and society as a serious emotional disorder. Erich Fromm further elaborated on this theme when he spoke of such personality types as the "hoarders, exploiters and marketers." An intense need to control others, a proclivity for inducing guilt and dependency in others, a marked selfishness, and insensitivity are no less problematic than schizophrenia; in fact, sometimes more so.

However, to deny that there is any such thing as mental illness shows a lack of common sense. At times such a denial can deprive a patient's family of some understanding of what they are going through. The father of an adolescent boy who had been hospitalized for three years related this experience: "When my son first became ill, he was only thirteen. He was depressed and attempted suicide. His behavior was strange, like mumbling incoherently to himself. I thought when he went into the hospital that he would be there only a few months. I did everything I could to cooperate with the doctors. I gave the social workers a complete history of my family.

"When I visited my son, I tried to do everything they told me . . . let him get angry at me if he wanted . . . avoid talking about things that might be upsetting. My wife and I were riddled with guilt. The longer the illness went on, the guiltier we felt. I tried to find out what was wrong from the doctors, but they talked with me only in terms of family relationships. I assumed that they thought my son's illness was the product of problems between my wife and me, and that we had done something awful to him during his childhood. It was two years later that I was finally told by a consulting doctor that he was suffering from a form of schizophrenia. He explained to me what that meant. For the first time I realized that a lot of things had gone into my son's illness—chemistry, genetics, things that might have happened during the pregnancy over which we could have had no control. It was the first time we felt any relief from the terrible guilt."

The careful use of diagnosis also provides a sound basis for medical treatment. Depression is not only a mood; it is also a diagnosis. For a select group of patients—the severely depressed and those with manic-depressive reactions—the diagnosis is vitally important in studying the causes of the condition and bringing effective treatment to bear on it.

To maintain that there is no such thing as mental illness contradicts the fact that throughout history special groups of individuals have been described whose symptoms correspond to current concepts of the more severe mood disorders and the schizophrenias, whatever they may have been called at the time. In 1620 at the University of Basel in Switzerland, Fridericus Flacht, later to become official physician for the City of Worms, published his *Treatise on Melancholia*. "Depression is an alienation of the mind," he wrote; ". . . such men often [shed] tears without any cause; others [laugh] uproariously. One thinks the Heavens will fall; another thinks himself to be a clay vessel, hence he carefully avoids contact with men, lest he be broken. . . . Fear and sorrow [last] for a long time without an obvious cause. . . . [There are] other types of madness as Mania . . . those especially seized upon by Mania with the greatest boldness and rage do not hesitate to attack anything threatening. . . .

"Another [man] imagined his buttocks to be made of crystal and hence whatever he had to do, he carried out in a standing position, fearing that if he sat down the structure of his buttocks would disintegrate into a thousand fragments."

The early physicians did not distinguish between various types of mental disorders, but clumped them all under one label: melancholia. It was not until the latter part of the nineteenth century that clinicians began to differentiate more carefully between the various forms of mental illness. From the disorders called melancholia, the Swiss neurologist Eugen Bleuler extracted the group he termed the schizophrenias. His definition of schizophrenia was based on the presence of certain signs and symptoms that included a serious disruption in the logical processes of thinking; a separation of the intellectual from the emotional processes, so that the individual might be thinking about sad and upsetting ideas with an external appearance of indifference; an autistic involvement in the person's own perception of reality, providing him with the ability to define his world according to his delusions; and a profound ambivalence in the way he experienced himself and the outer world. Schizophrenia thus defined actually has nothing to do with the popular concept of the split personality, as exemplified by the title characters of *Three Faces of Eve* and *Sybil*, both of whom represent hysterical personalities. The role played by Peter O'Toole in the film *The Ruling Class*, however, represents a classical form of schizophrenia, even though the film's irony again raises the question as to who is really sane and who is not.

The schizophrenias are divided into four subgroups. The simple type, which usually begins in early adolescence, may proceed to a state of apathy and deterioration within a decade. The hebephrenic, the popular concept of insanity, is characterized by hallucinations and by silly, inappropriate behavior, laughing, giggling, and grimacing without any obvious cause. The paranoid type generally starts later in life, in the mid-twenties, and is characterized by loosely defined but usually powerful delusions of persecution, often associated with auditory hallucinations. Finally, the catatonic type is typified by the mute, motionless patient who assumes statuelike postures for days or weeks as a way of withdrawing into his autistic world, rejecting external reality out of disappointment and rage; occasionally this withdrawal may be broken by episodes of agitated, destructive behavior called excitements.

In severe states of elation and depression, known as the manic-depressive reaction, a close relationship exists between the mood and thought processes of the patient that is lacking in schizophrenic patients. In 1899 the German psychiatrist Emil Kraepelin established the diagnosis of manic-depressive psychosis, a disorder in which a change in mood was of primary importance; that is, where the thinking processes of the patient were intact and the content of his thinking followed logically from the basic mood. If elated, the patient's exuberance affected his ideas, and his extravagant behavior stemmed from his spirits. If depressed, his preoccupation with morbid concerns reflected his hopelessness.

Kraepelin described the clinical signs of the manic-depressive reaction, including the predictability of its periodic quality. At certain seasons of the year, particularly spring and fall, such individuals would enter into episodes of elation or depression for no apparent reason. The rhythmic nature of the mood changes suggested that a biological clock within the patient determined when and for what period of time his mood might remain altered. Kraepelin's description of the manic-depressive patient is still valid, and subsequent research has indicated an important genetic factor in such conditions, as well as metabolic changes that include a tendency for sodium to be retained within the cells of the nervous system during episodes of disturbance.

John Traynor was forty-seven when his father died. For a week or so after the funeral he seemed quieter, more withdrawn than usual. Then, without warning, he purchased a valuable painting from a gallery for $11,000, a price he could ill afford. A few weeks later he began calling up his friends and neighbors, suggesting that they get together to form a committee that would raise several million dollars. The purpose: to rebuild the downtown section of the city in keeping with its nineteenth-century traditions. He also signed a pledge for fifty thousand dollars for the local community chest drive.

Neither his wife nor his attorney was able to deter him from his overactive behavior. Whenever they tried to speak with him he became enraged, threatening to divorce his wife and fire his lawyer. When his wife

arrived home one afternoon to find him in the library
with the telephone torn from its socket, screaming that
someone had tapped his phone to learn about a new
invention he had developed, she called the family doctor in a panic, and they arranged for him to be admitted to a psychiatric hospital.

Instead of entering a grief reaction after his father's death, Traynor had become elated, buoyant,
boisterous, full of himself and full of grand schemes
and ideas. He manifested a sharp sense of humor. He
became easily enraged. At the height of his elation, he
had become delusional. He was diagnosed as suffering
from a manic-depressive reaction, a condition which
affects about three or four people out of one thousand.

In the hospital, he was given phenothiazine medi-
cations. Within a few days his manic excitement began
to subside. By the end of the second week, however, he
was profoundly depressed and sat in his room, refusing
to come out. He would not speak with the doctors or
nurses. On one occasion he attempted to hang himself
on the closet door with his towel. Given a series of
eight electric convulsive treatments, he improved rapidly during the course of treatment and by the end
showed no signs of either elation or depression.

He remained in good condition for four years.
Sometimes he seemed a bit down, and at other times he
was more energetic and active than usual. These swings
seemed to have a rhythm about them, being more noticeable around the time of the anniversary of his first
episode. Then, abruptly and without warning, he became deeply depressed despite no apparent change in
his life situation. He made a serious, impulsive suicide

attempt, tying a stone around his waist and jumping into his swimming pool. He was hospitalized again at once.

This time he was given tricyclic antidepressants, which had been discovered during the years subsequent to his previous illness. His depression slowly lifted. He remained in fairly even spirits for another few weeks, but gradually he became euphoric, over-talkative and demanding. "I didn't intend to kill myself. Why should I when I have everything to live for? There is so much joy in the world. And I have found a way of feeling that joy. No, I won't tell you. It's a secret. You might find a way of taking it away from me."

By now he was very much elated and frankly delusional. The doctors started him on lithium, and over the next two weeks his elation subsided. Within two months he was well enough to be discharged from the hospital. He has been receiving lithium for the last five years and has had no recurrence of either elation or depression.

John Traynor exemplifies the importance of diagnosis in the small group of patients for whom such treatments as lithium or electric convulsive treatments may be indicated; that is, for a very severe state of elation or depression. However, not all severe states of depression are contained within the manic-depressive category. Psychiatrists, following Kraepelin's lead, made further attempts to clarify the various types of depressions that can occur. Some divided mood disorders into the exogenous type, in which external events in the patient's life could be identified as triggering the reaction, and the endogenous type, in which no such external changes could be detected. The former were said to be psychogenic in origin, the latter biochemical. As it became apparent that such rigid lines served little useful purpose and in fact tended to add fuel to the conflict between the psychologically oriented psychiatrists and the organicists, this distinction faded.

Other attempts at classification included the identification of the depression in terms of the period of life in which it occurred, along with the concomitant life changes: hence such terms were coined as involutional melancholia and depression of the aging period. Again, these distinctions were of little practical value and, if anything, led erroneously to the assumption that depression was primarily a reaction of middle-aged and elderly people, associated with menopause, the male climacteric, and the aging process.

Certain subgroupings, however, proved valuable, since they served as important clues to treatment—for example, the paranoid type of depression. Anyone who is depressed will feel hypersensitive and easily rejected. If the lack of trust accompanying this sensitivity becomes sufficiently intense, the person may become paranoid, even delusional.

In mild forms, the paranoid quality can be quite confusing to friends and relatives. "My wife has been accusing me of having an affair," said the husband of one depressed woman. "I can't get her off the subject. Of course, I haven't. I've never played around in twenty years of marriage. But, all of a sudden, she thinks I'm a son of a bitch. When I had to shorten our vacation from ten days to a week this summer, she had a fit. Said I was doing it to hurt her; that I didn't love her any more, or if I did, that I didn't know how to care about anyone except myself."

In more severe forms the paranoid element is quite evident. A thirty-year-old engineer had an argument with one of his close friends one evening. The next day he was quite depressed and did not go to work. By that evening he began to imagine that his mail was being intercepted and that people were spying on him from a neighboring house. He couldn't sleep at all that night. By the next day he was so frightened and agitated that his wife had to call the family physician, who arranged to hospitalize him. On a regime of therapy which included phenothiazines and antidepressants, his paranoid delusions subsided within a few days. However, his underlying depression became more pronounced, lasting for another four weeks before it finally lifted.

The diagnosis—a depression with paranoid features—alerted the physician to the importance of adding phenothiazine tranquilizers to the antidepressant treatment program in order to reduce the fear and agitation that were giving rise to his paranoid delusions. With the rapid growth in biochemical approaches to treatment, diagnosis, accompanied by a careful evaluation of the emotions and symptoms of the depression, has an important place in psychiatry. It permits the physician to select more accurately the right treatment for the right patient at the right time, particularly when he is attempting to accelerate the process of psychotherapy with antidepressant drugs, or to relieve intense states of depression with electric shock treatment.

Electric shock treatments were originally discovered by accident, when the Hungarian psychiatrist L. J. von Meduna attempted in 1935 to use convulsions in the treatment of schizophrenic patients. He believed that there was a low incidence of epilepsy among schizophrenic patients, and that epileptic patients rarely developed the symptoms of schizophrenia. This assumption, later disproved, led to his hypothesis that the induction of a series of grand mal convulsions, of the type characteristic of epilepsy, might have beneficial effects in schizophrenic patients. While some improvement in the condition was noted, the fundamental change produced by the convulsions appeared to be in mood, whether depression or elation. Subsequent investigations with depressed patients clarified the impression that a series of about six shock treatments would dramatically eliminate the mood disorder.

Giving electric shock treatment is a relatively simple procedure. In a special treatment room the patient receives anesthesia and muscle relaxants. Once asleep, he receives a sufficient amount of electrical current via two electrodes, one attached to each temple, to induce what is technically known as a grand mal seizure, which resembles an epileptic convulsion. There are, however, few, if any, bodily movements, since they are blocked by the use of the muscle relaxants given with the anesthesia. After the convulsion, which lasts less than a minute, the patient will sleep for an hour or more, and when he awakens he will usually not recall anything of the treatment itself.

Curiously, the therapeutic effects of the electric shock treatments do not depend on the actual physical manifestations of the convulsion. By the same token, the electricity is not relevant either. Inhalants—gases that can be given to produce convulsions—have the same therapeutic effect. The procedure works somehow by lowering the seizure threshold of the central nervous system and by inducing an associated shift in the metabolic balance of minerals and biogenic amines within the cells and at the cell membranes.

Although phenothiazines, lithium, and tricyclic antidepressants have markedly reduced the need for electric shock treatments, a certain number of patients still respond more adequately to shock than to these drugs, particularly those people who are both schizophrenic and depressed. Moreover, electric shock treatments work more quickly and with more guaranteed effectiveness. Hence they are still often used in patients who are intensely disturbed—for example, those who represent serious and immediate suicidal risks.

The rapid relief of symptoms by means of shock treatments, however, can discourage patient and doctor alike from exploring the psychological and environmental factors relevant to the depression. This often leaves the patient unprotected against a future recurrence of his mood disturbance. To many, the procedure itself sounds "brutal," although the physical complications of shock treatments are fewer and less serious than those incurred in performing a routine appendectomy. Many psychoanalytically oriented psychiatrists suggest that the treatments do nothing biologically, but rather submit the patient to a punitive experience whereby his guilt is expiated and his masochistic needs are temporarily fulfilled.

Most people are understandably reluctant to

allow themselves to be helplessly wheeled into a treatment room where anesthesia will render them unconscious and a group of doctors and nurses will then perform a procedure that alters the chemical and electrical balance of their brains. As a result of the aversion on the part of doctors to give the treatment as well as on the part of patients to receive it, there undoubtedly have been many occasions when shock treatments should have been used, but were not. On the other hand, the doctrine of therapeutic exclusiveness encouraged abuses of electric shock. Certain physicians felt that all emotional problems were rooted in biological causes, and some hospitals became "shock" mills where, whatever the condition and whatever its causes, the patient ended up receiving electric shock.

The use of lithium is another biological form of treatment in which the diagnosis of the patient is a critical factor. Lithium is effective in reducing the manic phase of the manic-depressive reaction. Furthermore, it probably prevents the patient from entering recurrent episodes of elation or depression. But it has no known effect in either relieving depression or preventing mood swings in patients who are not diagnosed as manic-depressive.

The indisputable effectiveness of biological methods of treatment in many patients with mood disorders underscores the importance of searching actively for an understanding of biochemical changes in brain function that in some instances go along with being depressed, and in others may actually cause the depression.

16

A
Biological
Basis
for
Depression

A NUMBER OF SCHOOLS OF THOUGHT have evolved over
the years within the fields of psychology and psychiatry, ranging from the orthodox Freudian position to
the Harry Stack Sullivan theories of interpersonal relationships; from Frederick Perl's gestalt approaches to
Skinnerian conditioning to the use of electric convulsive treatments by the organicists. Characteristic of
most schools, and of many of their practitioners, is an
absolutism, a conceptual and therapeutic exclusiveness.

"Depression is rooted in traumatic childhood experiences taking place during the oral and anal phases
of development, and only a thoroughgoing analysis
can modify the influence of this underlying structure
on the personality," states the Freudian analyst. "As
long as a person cannot experience himself in relation

to other members of the group and develop freedom in expressing feelings without fear of rejection, he cannot liberate himself from depression," a proponent of group therapy and encounter groups emphasizes. The psychiatrist Lothar Kalinowsky, in his text *Pharmacological, Convulsive and Other Somatic Treatments*, states simply that the depressed patient will usually respond to a series of six to eight electrically induced convulsions administered at the rate of two or three weekly.

To the average person, this variety of theories and practices can be quite confusing. How can a drug such as an antidepressant relieve a condition caused by the trauma experienced in going through a divorce? On the other hand, how can twenty sessions with a psychotherapist relieve depression if it is caused by something in the brain or the endocrine system?

The answer lies in visualizing the human being as a psychobiological unit. He is a physical and psychological organism in whom heredity, childhood experiences, adult personality characteristics, his interaction with his environment, the anticipated and unanticipated happenings in his life, and the nature of his central nervous system and hormone glands act synergistically to determine how he will respond to a given stress at a given moment in time. To understand this integration more thoroughly and the relevance of antidepressant medication to the depressed person's resilience—or lack of it—in rebounding from his mood, it is essential to consider the evidence for biochemical influences on depression.

There is as yet no unifying theory that explains

the variety of laboratory findings that link physiological changes with states of depression. Four main areas deserve attention: mineral metabolism, in particular calcium and sodium; endocrine metabolism, in particular thyroid and steroid function; central-nervous-system transmitters, in particular biogenic amines; and genetic determinants, of primary importance in the manic-depressive condition. I have selected for further discussion the investigations on calcium metabolism in depression which my colleagues and I conducted at the Payne Whitney Clinic—not because these findings are any more relevant than those indicating alterations in other biochemical or neurophysiological areas, but because the discussion will help clarify what is actually involved in this kind of research into the biochemical aspects of depression.

Considerable research on animal behavior has been carried out, especially with rhesus monkeys and mice. The obvious advantage in using animals is that the laboratory conditions offer greater experimental control and a wider variety of procedures than would be possible in experimenting with humans. The most serious limitation in such research, however, is that the discoveries cannot be transposed directly to man.

In the final analysis, it is the demonstration of biological changes in man himself that has the most direct relevance to human experience. In the area of behavior, this kind of study is uniquely difficult. It is not enough to say that such and such a chemical change has been observed in schizophrenic patients, for instance, since not all schizophrenic patients are alike. Some may not even be schizophrenic despite the medical diagnosis.

It is necessary, in other words, to define the parameters of behavior so that descriptive terms can be used with an adequate degree of reliability. If one is going to study depression, it is essential to define with some preciseness what signs and changes in the patient's behavior constitute depression, what other variables may confuse the picture, and with what reliability professional observers can agree in describing changes in behavior.

One way to avoid the mistake of comparing incomparables is to use the patient as his own control. In this way, because of biological variables from one person to another and the complex business of accurately rating behavior when many different patients and many different observers are involved, one of the soundest methods of evaluating physiological changes associated with swings in emotions and moods is to study these changes in the individual patient by observing particular biological functions at various phases in his condition to see how they compare. What can one say, for example, about calcium metabolism when the patient is depressed, and how does that compare with his calcium metabolism when he has recovered from the depression? Such an approach does not preclude the necessity of studying a sufficient number of patients in this way to allow for confirmation and broader generalization.

As with many other research findings, our discovery of a correlation between changes in depressed patients and calcium metabolism began in the setting of a related line of research. In 1955, on the metabolic unit of the Payne Whitney Clinic of the New York Hospital, we began to study biological aspects of psychiatric disorders. The study was originally designed to duplicate the findings of the Norwegian investigator Rolv Gjessing, who had demonstrated marked variations in the retention and excretion of nitrogen in certain schizophrenic patients who periodically and predictably entered and recovered from states of severe confusion. Gjessing had suggested that by blocking these changes in nitrogen metabolism by means of the thyroid hormone thyroxine, he had been able to prevent recurrences of the episodes of periodic catatonia.

Each of Gjessing's experiments took several years, since many months would elapse between and during each confusional episode. It occurred to us that if the confusional state could be interrupted in such patients by means of electric convulsive treatments (chlorpromazine and other major tranquilizers were only then coming into use), it might be possible to repeat his studies in a matter of a few months. But in order to interpret the results of such an approach, it would be necessary to know if the electric convulsive treatments themselves had any effect on the metabolic patterns to be studied.

Accordingly, a group of severely depressed patients who had been scheduled by their own doctors to receive shock treatments were transferred to the metabolic unit. There, each was placed on a controlled diet, carefully prepared by trained dieticians to ensure an adequate and regular daily intake of food substances. All urine and stool excretions were collected and sent daily to the unit's laboratories for determination of the amount of nitrogen, calcium, phosphorus, sodium, and potassium being excreted. By calculating the differences between the intake of these substances in the diet and their excretion from the body, it was possible to determine whether the patient was in a negative balance (losing the particular substance) or a positive balance (retaining the particular substance) and to what degree.

After at least a two-week control period, to obtain a base-line reading of the balances, the patients began their anticipated series of shock treatments. The balance studies continued without interruption. As the patients who improved recovered from depression, a remarkable change was noted. Nitrogen metabolism did not alter, nor did that of phosphorus, sodium, or potassium. But patient after patient showed a marked decrease in the urinary excretion of calcium and a significant increase in the amount of calcium retained by the body. The few depressed patients who did not improve showed no such calcium shift. Hence the calcium change seemed less related to the electric convulsive treatments than to the recovery from the depressed state.

Over the next few years, this impression was confirmed when a large number of depressed patients were studied before, during, and after the administration of the tricyclic antidepressant drug imipramine. The same shift in calcium metabolism occurred. Those who recovered revealed a substantial degree of calcium retention; those who did not showed no calcium changes.

The work continued. There was, of course, no way of knowing whether the calcium shifts were of central importance in depression, or only a relatively insignificant peripheral alteration reflecting other, more

relevant biochemical changes within the body. Theo-
retically, the calcium changes might be important,
since calcium is a major regulator of central-nervous-
system activity. Fluctuations in the amount of calcium
at the cell membranes affect the flow of substances in
and out of the cell—for example, the influx and efflux
of sodium ions. In addition, calcium is a nervous-sys-
tem "sedative": it reduces the excitability of the brain.
Abnormally low levels of calcium circulating in the
blood stream, as in hypoparathyroidism, can lead to
tetany and convulsions. Abnormally high levels of blood
calcium can produce confusion, coma, and even death.

Furthermore, calcium metabolism is clearly influenced by hormones, such as cortisone, that are known
to be involved in stress reactions. The adrenal gland
secretes large amounts of such steroids when the organism is under stress, and these in turn block the
absorption of calcium from the intestine. Physiologist
Hans Selye, in his description of stress responses,
pointed up the importance of calcium when he stated
that stress accelerates the aging process by activating
the removal of calcium from bone and its deposition in
soft tissues (where it does not belong).

The next question to be answered in our study
was: If calcium is being retained by the body during
the phase of recovery from depression, where is the
calcium going? The answer was obtained by carrying
out a series of studies involving the injection of the
radioactive isotope calcium-47 in a group of depressed
patients before and after treatment to track the movement of calcium in the body. It was discovered that the
retained calcium was going into bone. In the con-

tinual interchange of calcium that takes place within bone, and between bone and the rest of the body, the recovering patients revealed a decrease in the amount of calcium leaving bone and an increase in the amount of calcium being deposited in bone. At the same time, there seemed to be a slight decrease in the amount of calcium circulating in the blood stream.

The value of research often lies not so much in the answers obtained, but rather in the number of new questions the findings stimulate. What actually accounts for the calcium changes observed in depressed patients? Are they related to the depression itself, or are they connected with the phenomenon of recovery—with the rebounding from the tenacious hold of chronic depression? Does regular physical activity, which is believed to be associated with an increase in calcium retention, work to counteract depression and is it of curative value in those already caught in chronic depression?

Are there hormones, as yet undiscovered or untested, that might relieve depression or prevent it from becoming chronic? Thyrocalcitonin, for instance, a hormone formed in the thyroid gland that has been isolated and synthesized only within the last few years, causes a significant reduction in calcium excretion in animals and humans without affecting phosphorus metabolism and is now being evaluated as a treatment for Paget's disease, a bone disorder. In view of the observed connection between depression and calcium metabolism, thyrocalcitonin may prove to possess a significant antidepressant effect. The administration of thyroid hormones and the thyroid-stimulating hormone (a pituitary-gland hormone that regulates the amount of thyroid hormones produced by the thyroid gland) have already been shown to induce mild, though transitory, relief from depressive moods.

Is there a psychosomatic link between depression and various bone diseases, such as osteoarthritis, osteoporosis, and osteomalacia? Would it be possible to treat a condition such as osteoporosis, in which bone loses its calcium and its strength, with certain antidepressant drugs to effect a return of calcium to bone?

Does diet affect mood? In Colombia, South America, there are two cities that show a sharply different intake of calcium. The people of Medellín have a relatively low intake of calcium in their diet (360 milligrams daily), whereas the people of Bogotá have a significantly higher intake (860 milligrams daily). Is there a material difference in the incidence of depression between these two communities?

Fluorides, which have been placed in many water supplies throughout the world to reduce dental decay, have been shown in laboratory studies with animal tissues to influence the biochemical activity of calcium and other minerals, as well as biogenic amines. An extensive review of the fluoride literature reveals a singular lack of attention paid to the effects of fluorides on the central nervous systems of either animals or humans, and on the emotional and behavioral patterns of subjects ingesting large amounts of fluorides. Would the incidence of depression differ between a community with a fluoridated water supply and one without fluoridation?

Do the observed changes in calcium metabolism

in depressed patients relate to changes in other biochemical factors that have been reported by such investigators as Alec Coppen and Joseph Schildkraut? Coppen demonstrated that in both phases of manic-depressive reactions, sodium seemed to be retained within the cells of the central nervous system. This retention was noted only among patients with bipolar (true manic-depressive) reactions; it was not seen in unipolar depressions (those lacking a manic phase). His findings suggest a possible explanation for the value of lithium in the treatment and prevention of manic episodes in such patients. Presumably, lithium replaces the sodium within the cells and thereby prevents abnormal accumulations of the latter. Calcium regulates the flow of sodium across cell membranes. Variations in the amount of calcium at the cell membrane could account for the accumulation of sodium within the cells.

Schildkraut and others have focused largely on the relationship between depression and the metabolism of biogenic amines (central-nervous-system transmitters). The high degree of research interest in the role of biogenic amines in mood disorders was triggered by the observation that reserpine, one of the early tranquilizers, precipitated severe depressions in many people who received it. At the same time, in a special group of depressed individuals, monoamine oxidase inhibitors, which are no longer in general use, appeared to produce a significant elevation in mood. Both compounds affect the amount of the biogenic amine norepinephrine in the brain. In particular, it is hypothesized that depressed patients have an insufficient amount of norepinephrine at synaptic clefts within the central nervous system and that biological treatment restores this level to normal. A connection between the changes in calcium metabolism and the biogenic amine hypothesis has yet to be established.

What is important for the average person to be aware of is the existence of a growing body of evidence —some of it empirical, such as the effectiveness of drugs in relieving chronic depression, some of it the result of basic scientific investigations—that indicates a considerable biological basis for depression. Furthermore, the need to investigate biological factors that influence mood and behavior has become more urgent than ever as the complexities of modern society place greater stresses on everyone.

The biological aspects of depression do not preclude the importance of environmental or interpersonal elements, for it is essential to view the human being as a whole, mind and body, inner world and outer world, acting, reacting, and interacting.

17

The
Best
Healing
Is
Prevention

TREATMENT AFTER THE FACT is never as effective as prevention. "The best healing," the official Physician for the City of Worms wrote in 1620 in reference to melancholia, "would be to work at foresight." The prevention of depression, however, is more complex than the prevention of other human ailments. It does not mean the elimination of sadness, as Aldous Huxley proposed with Soma in his satire *Brave New World.* Everyone is going to experience some despondency at one time or another in his life. "'Tis most absurd and ridiculous," commented Robert Burton in his *Anatomy of Melancholy,* "for any mortal man to look for a perpetual tenor of happiness in his life."

What the prevention of depression does mean is the avoidance of chronic depression and the traps that the chronically depressed person is liable to construct. It involves experiencing depression directly rather than denying it and converting it into other physical, psychological, or behavioral channels. It means resolving, within a person and his environment, conflicts that make him depressed when he needn't be.

These goals require a change in public attitudes, so that people who are depressed will know how and where to find professional help when they need it, and will do so without delay and embarrassment. In a more basic way, prevention involves creating educational programs of various types to strengthen our abilities to cope more effectively with life stresses. It is no longer practical to leave such learning to chance. The demands of living in our rapidly changing society are too great and too complex to hope that we can meet them successfully just by muddling through.

To the extent that depression can be considered a health problem, its prevention can be divided into three phases: tertiary, secondary, and primary.

Tertiary prevention involves steps that can be taken to prevent the person who has pulled out of a depression from slipping back into it again. One of the fundamental goals of therapy is to modify his value system and his methods of coping with stress so as to eliminate patterns of behavior that set him up for depression—procrastination and denial, for example. The depressed person puts off dealing with situations that are difficult or unpleasant. He does not sit down quietly with his wife to talk about ways of improving their sexual life. She does not set aside some time to bring to her husband's attention important differences in their attitudes toward raising the children. Instead, critical issues are submerged, pushed underground, ignored. To avoid becoming depressed again, such an individual must learn how to be more alert to issues as they arise and to deal more directly with them.

In fostering the growth of family therapy, psychiatrists Nathan Ackerman and Ronald D. Laing have made a major contribution to tertiary prevention. No one is depressed by himself. The depressed person is a particular individual in a particular life situation. He has an impact on his family and co-workers, and they in turn have an important impact on him. They may have contributed substantially to his having become depressed; or, confronted with his depression, they may either aggravate it or offer him empathy and support.

The willingness of key family members to cooperate with the patient's therapy has almost become a prognostic factor in evaluating the eventual outcome of the depression as well as of the family interactions. The husband who refuses to see his wife's psychiatrist when requested to do so may be concealing something —an extramarital affair, for example—or he may be fearful of losing some degree of control over her as a result of successful therapy. The wife who cannot bring herself to cooperate with therapy may feel embarrassed or guilty, with or without cause, about her complicity in provoking the depression, and at the same time she may lack the insight and flexibility required to change a long-standing habit of psychological sabotage. On the whole, the more cooperative and sincere the family members are, the easier it is for the depressed person to recover and remain free of depression.

There are times when a depression accompanies a major change in a person's life and when his recovery and readjustment demand a reorientation and new way of living, as in divorce or the death of a husband or wife. Then the individual must face a new kind of existence—the world of the widow or widower, or the world of the formerly married.

"After the divorce," one man said, "I became so depressed I had to go into a psychiatric hospital for a couple of months. There were times I wanted to kill myself. I was scared and lonely. The worst part of it was over in a few weeks, but the awful loneliness, the aching for someone to be close to, for a home, went on for months. I can remember lying in bed at night sometimes, fighting against the urge to rush to the window and jump out.

"After I left the hospital, I went back to work, and that helped. I saw plenty of my children and that helped, too. My friends invited me to a few parties. I met a couple of girls, but no one that really interested me. The doctor kept telling me that at forty-four I would be a popular guest at dinner and that I'd have no trouble meeting women. That was a lot of crap. I spent most of my time in the apartment, reading and watching television. I took some trips. One night I went to a singles' bar, but that was really depressing. What the hell are you supposed to do?"

Too few concrete opportunities exist for people faced with such a crisis. Parents Without Partners, an organization that brings together divorced or widowed parents to help them share with each other the problems of raising children alone, is one such effort. Much more often the recovered individual is uninformed about the opportunities that do exist and how to make the best use of them.

Secondary prevention deals with the continuing education of the professional and with the alerting of the public to the nature of depression so that those who need help can seek it as soon as possible. The lack of adequate training in psychiatry for the nonpsychiatric physician has been one of the more serious stumbling blocks in the secondary prevention of depression. Prior to the mid-1950s, the majority of medical schools did not have departments of psychiatry. The teaching programs that then existed often failed to make psychiatry relevant to the practice of medicine, and the physician was left with the idea that psychiatry was either a specialty devoted to the treatment of the insane, or a hodgepodge of theories founded on the observations of Freud and his followers. As a result the medical student often concluded that a doctor should call in a psychiatrist only when the patient had one foot out of the window or was insisting on some kind of psychiatric help.

Paradoxically, the family physician is often the first to be exposed to depression in his patients, since the depressed individual may experience his depression as a physical ailment. "When I had my first attack of panic," said a forty-two-year-old auto mechanic, "I was convinced that I was having a heart attack. I went to my doctor, who did a series of tests. He told me that there was nothing wrong; and since he couldn't make a diagnosis, he suggested that I take some tranquilizers and go on a vacation. It didn't work. I was sure he had missed the diagnosis, so I went to another doctor, who came up with the same opinion. Finally I found one who explained to me that my chest pains and palpitations were signs of tension and depression and did something about it."

The continuing education of the psychiatrist and other professionals involved in therapy and counseling is equally important. Over the past decade more and more people are practicing therapy; they come from a variety of backgrounds and have many different skills and points of view. The psychiatrist who was trained as recently as ten years ago faces the need to constantly update his knowledge as new approaches to treatment are introduced—gestalt therapy, transcendental meditation, encounter groups, behavior therapy, community mental health center programs, new psychopharmacologic agents.

Psychologists and social workers, now working extensively in private practice and in outpatient departments, often require additional training in the techniques of brief psychotherapy and knowledge of the criteria for using antidepressant drugs and tranquilizers. The clergy are also actively involved in counseling. One minister had been seeing a parishioner twice a week for nearly two years, trying to help her deal with a difficult marriage, before he recognized that her over-all lack of progress was caused by chronic depression. He then referred her to a physician for supplemental antidepressant drug treatment.

While the upgrading of professional skills is an

essential part of secondary prevention, equally important are improvements in insurance coverage that will encourage people to obtain the professional help they need as early as possible, rather than waiting until the complications of depression overshadow the condition itself.

Many firms select major health policies for their employees that exclude or seriously limit coverage for outpatient psychiatric care. The coverage for psychiatric hospital care is usually better, as high as 80 per cent of the cost of treatment up to a maximum of $15,000 to $25,000. This arrangement, of course, makes it cheaper for the patient to be hospitalized for the treatment of depression than to seek it on an outpatient basis. The implication of such a policy is that therapy is somehow fraudulent unless one is extremely disturbed. Its net effect is that many people will wait until they are sufficiently disturbed to require hospitalization before getting the help that would have prevented things from getting out of hand. A reconsideration of how insurance programs can more effectively encourage prevention is drastically needed.

Primary prevention is concerned with two major goals: first, to increase the public's awareness of the best ways to cope with appropriate episodes of acute depression; and secondly, to teach the individual ways to avoid becoming caught in chronic depression or in depressogenic environments.

If we consider some of the basic causes of depression—sensitivity to loss and rejection, lack of self-esteem, difficulty in recognizing and mobilizing emotions and in being constructively aggressive, conflicts about dependency, multiple stresses and long-term exposure to depressogenic environments—it is possible to begin defining the kinds of approaches required for primary prevention.

Because, for example, a healthy sense of self and the proper balance between self-reliance and dependency are formed during infancy and childhood, the learning process is heavily conditioned by the quality of the relationship between the mother and her child. What is being done, then, to educate young women in raising children? One of the things a mother should be alert to is the tendency of all parents to repeat—unintentionally—many of the errors made by their own parents during their upbringing. This problem may be concealed behind conscious efforts to do the exact opposite.

One woman, the mother of three teen-agers, consulted a social worker because of their apathetic and sometimes belligerent behavior. The mother herself had deliberately taken steps to promote her children's independence, or so she thought, and was disturbed to see the extent to which they lacked initiative and clung to the family. In fact, she had been doing the very opposite. One summer, for instance, when she sent her daughter to camp, she said: "It will do you good to get away from home for a while. It will help you stand on your own two feet." She added, however, "I'm not going to visit you. I couldn't bear having to say good-by again." In thousands of small ways, verbally and nonverbally, she had been simultaneously pushing her children toward greater freedom and pulling them back into a more dependent position.

Her pattern so resembled her mother's that when she fully realized it she was astonished. Her mother had surreptitiously encouraged her children to remain dependent on her long after they had married and begun to raise their own families. Both daughters had placed her well-being ahead of the well-being of their husbands and, at times, ahead of that of their own children.

One alternative to such a problem—a mother discovering that her children have reached adolescence unprepared to break away—is for her to prepare herself more adequately to manage her child's psychological development. The New York chapter of the Junior League has recently initiated a discussion-workshop program in which expectant mothers and mothers of newborns can sharpen their knowledge of, and intuition about, raising children. Men, too, in this society are confused and anxious about their roles as parents and could also benefit from professionally designed programs that would help them be more effective and comfortable with themselves as fathers.

Another concept in primary prevention—"fight clinics"—has been advanced by psychiatrist George Bach. His thesis is simple. Unless men and women living together in the close proximity of marriage and family life can learn how to disagree, argue, discharge hostile emotions, and come to terms with each other, at best there can be no intimacy, and at worst normal grievances and difficulties may pile up to crisis proportions or induce chronic depression in one partner or both.

Channeling hostility constructively is only one

aspect of improving communication. Good communication implies much more than that, and is an important part of preventing depression. Several years ago *Life* magazine ran an article that asked: If you were unhappy and in trouble at three o'clock in the morning, whom could you call? A mildly depressed person can at times be driven to the point of panic and despair simply for the want of someone with whom he can share what he is going through—someone who can be empathetic, someone who can listen, someone who can maintain perspective when he has lost his, someone he can trust.

A thirty-three-year-old woman was profoundly unhappy after the death of her sister, who had been suffering from multiple sclerosis. After the funeral, she could not sleep through the night and felt guilty that she had not done more to make her sister comfortable in the last days of her life. "I should have been there when she died; she must have been so lonely and afraid."

She was unable to express her feelings to anyone close to her. She did not want to tell her mother how upset she was, since her mother was also distressed. She tried to communicate her guilt and sadness to her husband, but he became impatient with her. "There's nothing to be so upset about," he replied abruptly. "You did all you could. You have to stop thinking about it."

Finally she consulted her minister, a trained counselor. In less than an hour she was able to talk about her feelings. She cried, and afterward felt much better for having shared her sorrow with someone who understood. But the question remained: Why had she not been able to confide in her husband? Why did he reject her feelings of depression?

The minister asked to see the couple together. In the session, the extent of the husband's dependency on his wife's good spirits became apparent. "When she is upset or cries, it agitates me. I'm really not angry with her. I can't stand any feelings of depression in myself. They frighten me—although I've never really thought about it until now."

The women's liberation movement is also making a contribution to the primary prevention of depression. A common setting for depression has been menopause. For numerous reasons—some physical and psychological, some environmental—many women become depressed in their late forties and early fifties. They feel that they are losing the youthful attractiveness overvalued in this society. It is the time when they find their children grown, their husbands busily engaged in work, and themselves without purpose or direction. It is the time for them to feel lonely, lost, useless, depressed.

By encouraging women to better define themselves as individuals before getting married, and to preserve that identity within the framework of marriage—to enter an I-Thou relationship with their husbands without losing the "I" in the process—women's liberation is offering a sensible way to avoid chronic depression. In this way, a woman will not only have more respect for herself and will have cultivated more avenues for self-expression and fulfillment, but she will also be less dependent on her role of wife and mother and on her youthfulness to provide her with a sense of identity and purpose.

Any popular movement, however, can be misused by some people in the service of their own personal problems. In its efforts to alert women to some of their needs and to improve their opportunities, "women's lib" has tapped the reservoir of frustrations that exist within every human being. Millions of women who may be unhappy or unfulfilled for a variety of reasons have now become convinced that their problems stem primarily from the injustices they have experienced because of being women. They are encouraged to turn against their families and their husbands in an effort to solve difficulties that do not legitimately originate in those areas. They get angry at the wrong person for the wrong reasons at the wrong time.

A forty-one-year-old man consulted a psychiatrist because of tension and feelings of hopelessness that he attributed to a major change in his relationship with his wife. They had been married for twelve years and had three children. Four years earlier his wife had become actively interested in the women's liberation movement. He had encouraged her interest and had participated with her in attending meetings and discussion groups. During the year preceding his first consultation with the therapist, she had become involved in an affair with a neighbor and had made no effort to conceal it. "I have a right to find my own fulfillment. We have a new kind of marriage," she stated. "No, I don't want a divorce or a separation, and I don't see why you do. After all, men have been doing this kind of thing for a long time. Why can't women?"

When his wife came to see the consultant, reluctantly and only to "help give information that might straighten my husband out," she revealed a good deal of confusion and a façade of bravado erected to protect her against feelings of depression. Her real conflict was not with her husband but with her alcoholic mother, who alternately depended on her and abused her. When she was getting along well with her husband in the early years of her marriage, she had many open confrontations with her mother and felt guilty about them. When she was able to control her feelings toward her mother and that relationship was smoother, she found herself in an angry power struggle with her husband—a response consistent with Freud's observation in his paper "Female Sexuality" (1931) that women tend to project onto their husbands conflicts originally experienced in their relationships with their mothers. Her growing interest in "women's lib" distracted her from the real issue—a complex problem of her interaction with her mother—and instead fanned a defensive resentment against her husband.

Prevention calls for ways in which the individual can learn how to discriminate between the influences of a changing society and what his own personal situation requires. It calls for better ways of coping with stress.

Coping can be taught in the home, at work, in the classroom. One of the first attempts to introduce formal mental health education into a school curriculum was made in 1944 in Toms River, New Jersey. A course in family relationships was given to junior and senior high school students on an elective basis. In lectures and seminars the youngsters were able to explore their expectations of marriage and their ideas on choosing marriage partners, and to learn ways and means of handling conflicts arising within marriage. An evaluation of the effects of the program on the group several years later revealed an impressively low incidence of divorce and family difficulties. Commenting on this program, psychiatrist David Levy, then a member of the Committee on Preventive Psychiatry of the Group for Advancement of Psychiatry, stated: "It is preventive psychiatry in the sense that it substitutes for haphazard experience a real preparation for family life, a reflective attitude, and a maturing process."

In recent years preventive programs have focused largely on children, on the assumption that character structure is formed during the first six years of life. While these years are vital and such an approach is invaluable, it should not distract us from the fact that a person's ability to meet life stresses successfully can be improved, in a planned way, at any age.

At Cornell University Medical College, for example, the first-year medical students are offered the opportunity to meet in groups of eight under the supervision of a psychiatrist to discuss the stresses in going through medical school and in becoming physicians. They not only have a chance to deal with the anxiety caused by both the nature and amount of work demanded of them, but they also have an opportunity to gain insight into emotional conflicts that may cause them difficulty in their later lives as physicians—the handling of anger and guilt, for example. Medical students, on the whole, have very high ideals that are difficult if not impossible to fulfill. They have a strong sense of responsibility that in the practice of medicine can make them especially vulnerable to unrecognized guilt and depression, as they are inevitably confronted year after year with the problems of chronic and fatal illness. The evidence of what unresolved conflicts can do to the individual physician can be seen even by the time he is about to graduate from medical school. He enters as an alert, energetic, and humanistic young man; four years later he already reveals a loss in his touch for human relationships, as well as in his flexibility and creativity.

The need for prevention is no less important to industry. Corporations will spend millions to prepare employees in the techniques of selling or in the practical aspects of management training, but they have yet to realize the potential profitability of programs designed to assist these employees in coping with such stressful changes as promotion, geographical shifts, retirement—changes that, if not adequately handled, can provoke depression. Depression is often at the root of problems with which industry is all too familiar—absenteeism and alcoholism.

In addition to paying attention to the needs of the individual, organizations should also consider ways of changing an environment which is depressogenic. During the last few years, many groups have used a variety of approaches, such as sensitivity training, to improve human relationships and communication. It was assumed, incorrectly, that the quality of the working environment would necessarily improve as a result. This did not follow. In fact, some very real problems arose when people who worked together in a competitive environment were expected to open up and reveal themselves to one another.

Although many individuals may have benefited from these sessions, the organization as a whole usually did not. This resulted from a failure to carefully define the nature, purpose, needs, and conflicts of the organization beforehand, and then apply methods, on a priority basis, to solve the most relevant issues.

A case in point was a small coeducational college where the dean found it difficult to hold on to bright, energetic young faculty members. They would come for a year or two and then leave, even though the financial benefits and living conditions were attractive. The dean requested a professional evaluation of the situation—a rather courageous and innovative step for him to take.

Over a two-month period of collecting and analyzing data, the consultants identified a central problem. A year before, a number of faculty members had participated in sensitivity training sessions, and while some found these personally helpful, the sessions did not significantly affect the over-all environment. What had not been detected at that time was a serious undercurrent of competitiveness among the department heads. Occasionally the competitiveness surfaced in the form of open conflict; for the most part, however, it took the form of an extensive lack of communication among the department heads and their subordinates and a consequent absence of collaboration. They had been asked to set up a new curriculum, but after a year of effort had not been able to do so. What appeared to be indifference was in fact a stubborn refusal to accept and admit the significance of one another's contributions.

The consultants designed a special program to deal with this problem. The fourteen department heads attended a four-day conference in which various group techniques such as game playing were used experimentally to teach the mechanics of effective collaboration. Divided into two groups of seven each, the participants were asked to find a common task which they could work on together and through which they could earn a living outside the academic world.

Under the supervision of the consultants, they proceeded to identify individual talents unrelated to their teaching roles. One group decided to open a resort hotel and assigned tasks to each member, ranging from cook to reservations clerk to public relations director. The other group decided to set up a travel agency and assigned appropriate roles to each member. They enjoyed the game and found it intrinsically rewarding.

Later, however, when they started to work on specific tasks that had to do with the curriculum itself, they again found it difficult to communicate and impossible to be innovative. With the help of the consultants, they could see, dramatically, the serious obstacles to collaboration that appeared when they had to work together on emotionally charged topics. Most important, they were able to experience and resolve some of the intense competitiveness that had been blocking communication.

The younger members of the faculty had not been

able to identify what it was that had made them un-happy and discontented. A dozen or more reasons had been put forth, but none was directed at the true cause of the problem. As a result of this special conference, the department heads were able to take a first step toward changing what had been a depressogenic environment.

Most people are not in a position to modify, by themselves, the over-all quality of the organizations within which they work. For many whose depressions are caused by a particular environment, there may be no option but to leave. Many men and women who change jobs, giving themselves various reasons for do-ing so, are, in fact, attempting to escape a depressogenic situation.

There is one place where the individual can do a great deal toward altering his environment, however, and that is within his own home. The basic principles involved are clear. If someone is depressed, he should consider what can be done to change those elements in family life that are contributing to his depression. If someone else in the family is depressed, what might others be doing or not doing to add to his distress? Such questions should be asked not with the idea of placing blame and focusing guilt, but rather with the hope of turning an unrewarding situation into a re-warding one and of making an already satisfactory condition even more so.

If you are trying to change yourself or your life situation, you are bound to experience depression. If you are already depressed, you have an opportunity to make progress in three major areas: how you regard yourself, how you relate to other people, and how you may modify and cope with difficult environmental conditions.

How you regard yourself. A research analyst commented: "Before my depression, I was always trying to win someone's approval. I worried about what my wife thought of me, what my employer thought of me, what impression I was making on other members of the department. I would go to almost any length to avoid being criticized. I needed constant feedback to reassure me that I was doing an adequate job.

"While I was depressed, none of this seemed to matter any more. For the first time I saw my craving for approval as a recurrent pattern, one that dominated my life. It seemed irrational. Couldn't I define myself for myself? Couldn't I know and sense the person I am? As long as I relied on the definition of myself through others, it was as if I had no identity of my own.

"Now that I'm not depressed any more, I'm different. I know my abilities, and I know my limitations. I still want to please, but I'm more selective about it."

Interpersonal relationships. A woman described the following change in her marriage: "Before my depression, neither my husband nor I was aware of the way in which we were competing with each other all over the place—for the children's attention, careerwise. I used to resent his successes so much that I wouldn't let him talk about his work at all. And I felt that he had no appreciation for what I was doing at home. It was so bad that we would sometimes compete with each other for the affection of my parents and his.

"But we weren't aware of it until the marriage nearly fell apart. My becoming depressed forced us to take a new look at what was going on between us. It was a shock to realize that competitiveness had been wrecking the love and respect we had for each other. It had even messed up our sex life.

"Now the one-upmanship is gone. It didn't just disappear, of course. But we're aware of it when it creeps in and we can correct it. When I was depressed, nothing mattered. Now that I'm not, I feel more able to share than I ever was."

And her husband commented, "We don't shove everything under the rug any more. I've learned to be more forthright, to say what I think and feel and try to say it so I can be understood. I wasn't as depressed as my wife, but I certainly was unhappy. I realized that things couldn't go on as they were. I would have to find new ways of dealing with issues, especially controversial ones, rather than passing them off time and time again."

Coping with difficult life situations. Aging, the time in life over sixty, can be a period of loneliness and unhappiness for many people. Retirement brings a halt to what is considered productive work. A sense of being useless moves in, and when idleness is compounded by health and financial problems, depression is common. "I used to lead a very active life," said one man. "Had my own consulting firm. I never was a roaring success, but we did well enough. Two years ago my partners insisted that I retire and gave me six months to do it in. At first I fought it. Then I gave in.

"My wife and I moved to Phoenix. We didn't know

anyone. Suddenly, after years of being up at six and working until seven and traveling everywhere, there was nothing for me to do. I dreaded the mornings. Going to buy *The New York Times* was the big event of the day. I lost interest in seeing anyone. Half the time I didn't want to eat. I was really morose and difficult to live with. I began to think there was something wrong with me physically.

"My family doctor assured me I was in good health. He made a few suggestions that proved invaluable—such as asking me what I had been interested in during my school years. I recalled that I would enter photography contests and that I had a rock collection. At one time I had even thought of being a geologist. Instead of sitting around thinking about doing things that didn't interest me, such as working for the local community chest, why didn't I pick up those old interests now that I had time to pursue them? I could feel myself coming alive again even as we talked about it."

How you regard depression depends on how you experience it. Because, by its very nature, it is associated with endings, and because each ending involves starting over, depression is itself a new beginning.

Selected
References

Akiskal, Hagop, and McKinney, William. "Depressive Disorders: Toward a Unified Hypothesis." *Science*, Vol. 182, No. 4107 (October 5, 1973), pp. 20–29.

Bach, George R., and Wyden, Peter. *The Intimate Enemy: How to Fight Pain in Love and Marriage*. New York: William Morrow, 1969.

Binswanger, Ludwig. *Being-in-the-World*. New York, London: Basic Books, Inc., 1963.

Bleuler, Eugen. *Dementia Praecox; or The Group of Schizophrenias*. New York: International Universities Press, 1950.

Blos, Peter. *On Adolescence: A Psychoanalytic Interpretation*. New York: The Free Press, 1962.

Burton, Robert. *The Anatomy of Melancholy*. Various editions.

Coppen, Alec. "Mineral Metabolism in Affective Disorders." *British Journal of Psychiatry*, Vol. 111 (1965), pp. 1133–42.

Diethelm, Oskar, and Flach, Frederic. "An Investigation of

the Psychopathologic Effect of Specific Emotions." *Experimental Psychopathology*, edited by Paul Henry Hoch and Joseph Zubin. New York: Grune & Stratton, 1957.

Duguay, Robert, and Flach, Frederic. "An Experimental Study of Weight Changes in Depression." *Acta Psychiatrica Scandinavica*, Vol. 40 (1964), pp. 1–9.

Erikson, Erik H. *Childhood and Society*. New York: W. W. Norton & Company, Inc., 1950.

Faragalla, Farouk, and Flach, Frederic. "Studies of Mineral Metabolism in Mental Depression." *Journal of Nervous and Mental Disease*, Vol. 151, No. 2 (1970), pp. 120–29.

Flach, Frederic. "The Use of Chlorpromazine to Facilitate Intensive Dynamic Psychotherapy in Depression." *Psychiatria et Neurologia*, Vol. 134, No. 5 (1957), pp. 289–97.

———. "Calcium Metabolism in States of Depression." *British Journal of Psychiatry*, Vol. 110, No. 467 (1964), pp. 588–93.

———. "Group Approaches in Medical Education." *Comprehensive Group Psychotherapy*, edited by Harold I. Kaplan and Benjamin J. Sadock. Baltimore: Williams & Wilkins, 1971.

———. "Depression: Key Factors in Diagnosis and Management." A Psychosonics Series for the Family Physician. New York: Mindex Communications, 1972. (An audio-cassette prepared under a grant from Merck, Sharp, and Dohme)

———, and Regan, Peter. *Chemotherapy in Emotional Disorders: The Psychotherapeutic Use of Somatic Treatments*. New York: McGraw Hill, 1960.

———, and Liang, Edward. "The Operation of a Metabolic Unit in Psychiatry." *Journal of Nervous and Mental Disease*, Vol. 136, No. 5 (1963), pp. 51–57.

———, and Draghi, Suzanne, eds. *The Nature and Treatment of Depression*. New York: John Wiley and Sons, Inc., forthcoming.

Flacht, Fridericus. "De Melancholia et Idiopathica et Sympathica." Basel: 1620.

Freud, Sigmund. "Mourning and Melancholia," 1917 (Vol. 4, pp. 152–70); "Female Sexuality," 1931 (Vol. 5, pp. 252–72); "Analysis Terminable and Interminable," 1937 (Vol. 5, pp. 316–57). In *The Collected Papers of Sigmund Freud*, edited by Ernest Jones (The International Psycho-Analytic Library). New York: Basic Books, Inc., 1959.

Fromm, Erich. *Man for Himself: An Inquiry into the Psychology of Ethics*. New York, Toronto: Rinehart & Co., Inc., 1947.

Kalinowsky, Lothar B., and Hippius, Hanns. *Pharmacological, Convulsive, and Other Somatic Treatments in Psychiatry*. New York, London: Grune & Stratton, 1969.

Kiev, Ari. *Transcultural Psychiatry*. New York: The Free Press, 1972.

Kohl, Richard, and Flach, Frederic. "Intensive Psychodynamic Treatment of Depressions." *Archives of Neurology and Psychiatry*, Vol. 72 (1954), pp. 383–84.

Kraepelin, Emil. *Manic-Depressive Insanity and Paranoia*. Edinburgh: E. & S. Livingstone, 1921.

Kubie, Lawrence S. *Neurotic Distortion of the Creative Process*. Lawrence, Kansas: University of Kansas Press, 1958.

————. "The Destructive Potential of Humor in Psychotherapy." *The American Journal of Psychiatry*, Vol. 127, No. 7 (1971), pp. 861–66.

Laing, Ronald D. *The Politics of the Family*. New York: Pantheon Books, 1971.

Lesse, Stanley. "The Multivariant Masks of Depression." *The American Journal of Psychiatry*, Vol. 124, No. 11, Supplement (1968).

Paykel, E. S., Myers, J. K., Dienelt, M. N., Klerman, G. L., Lindenthal, J. J. and Pepper, M. P. "Life Events and Depression." *Archives of General Psychiatry*, Vol. 21, No. 6 (1969), pp. 753–60.

Peter, Laurence J., and Hull, Raymond. *The Peter Principle:*

Why Things Always Go Wrong. New York: William Morrow, 1969.

Petersen, William. *Man, Weather, Sun.* Springfield, Illinois: Charles C. Thomas, 1947.

Redlich, Frederick C., and Hollingshead, August de Belmont. *Social Class and Mental Illness: A Community Study.* New York: John Wiley and Sons, 1958.

Reich, Wilhelm. *Character-Analysis.* New York: Orgone Institute Press, 1949.

Schildkraut, Joseph. "The Catecholamine Hypothesis of Affective Disorders: A Review of Supporting Evidence." *The American Journal of Psychiatry,* Vol. 122 (1965), pp. 509–22.

Sørenson, A., and Strömgren, E. "Frequency of Depressive States Within Geographically Delimited Population Groups." *Acta Psychiatrica Scandinavica* Supplement, Vol. 162, No. 62 (1962), pp. 62–68.

Index